PSYCHIC ABILITIES

PSYCHIC ABILITIES

How to Train and Use Them

MARCIA L. PICKANDS

SAMUEL WEISER, INC.
York Beach, Maine

First published in 1999 by
Samuel Weiser, Inc.
P. O. Box 612
York Beach, ME 03910-0612
www.weiserbooks.com

Library of Congress Cataloging-in-Publication Data

Pickands, Marcia L.
    Psychic abilities : how to train and use them / Marcia Pickands.
        p.   cm.
    Includes bibliographical references and index.
    ISBN 1-57863-111-4 (pbk. : alk. paper)
    1. Psychic ability.   I. Title.
    BF1031.P525   1999
    133.8—dc21   99-22982
                                                                          CIP

CCP

Typeset in 11 point Palatino

Image © 1999 Photodisc, Inc.
Cover design by Kathryn Sky-Peck
Interior illustrations by Tanith Pickands

Printed in the United States of America

08   07   06   05   04   03   02   01   00   99
10   9   8   7   6   5   4   3   2   1

The paper used in this publication meets the minimum requirements of
the American National Standard for Information Sciences—Permanence
of Paper for Printed Library Materials Z39.48–1992 (R1997).

This book is dedicated to those who have shared so much of their knowledge of these matters with me over the years: Daniel K. Pai (1930–1993), the late Grandmaster of Pai Lum (also known as White Dragon) Kung Fu; and William G. Gray (1913–1992), the founder of The Sangreal Sodality and author of many fine books on the Western Mystery Tradition.

TABLE OF CONTENTS

Exercises viii

Acknowledgments ix

Introduction xi

Chapter 1: How to Develop
Your Psychic Abilities 1

Chapter 2: Tarot as a Symbolic Language 13

Chapter 3: Numerology as a Symbolic Language 27

Chapter 4: Psychic Abilities
versus Spiritual Power 43

Chapter 5: How Psychic Readings Differ
from Divination 55

Chapter 6: Communicating with the Dead 63

Chapter 7: Responsible Use of Psychic Abilities 77

Chapter 8: Advanced Applications
of Psychic Abilities 105

Chapter 9: The World Needs You at Your Best! 115

Appendix: Additional Resources 127

Bibliography 129

Index 131

About the Author 133

EXERCISES

1. Centering 4

2. Grounding 5

3. Awakening Awareness
Within Your Physical Body 6

4. Psychically Sensing Time 8

5. Learning to See 9

6. Teaching Your *Conscious* Mind
the Meaning of Individual Tarot Cards 15

7. Teaching Your *Subsconcious* Mind
the Meaning of Individual Tarot Cards 16

8. Integrating Subconscious and Conscious
Meanings for Individual Tarot Cards 16

9. Daily Reading for Yourself 19

10. Reading Tarot Cards for Others 24

11. Casting and Analyzing Your Birth Name Chart . . . 33

12. Casting and Analyzing a Birthdate Chart 36

13. Accelerated Vision Quest 48

14. Consecrating a Tarot Deck
(or any tool) for the Purpose of Divination 56

15. A Simple Tarot Divination Method 59

16. Using a Ouija Board Instead of a Trance
Medium in a Protected, Séance-Like Setting 67

17. The Dumb Supper 71

18. What is Done to Your Invisible Body
Affects Your Visible/Physical Body 77

ACKNOWLEDGMENTS

I would like to especially thank several friends who shared their views of intuitive and human development with me for the purpose of this work: my adoptive sister, Marti Mom Feather Kaelbli, a Cherokee elder and spiritual leader; James Walks With Old Ones O'Loughlin, a Cherokee/ Shawnee Medicine Man; and Brian Standing Bear Wilkes, a Cherokee teacher.

Finally, many thanks to my husband, Martin Pickands, without whose help this book could never have been completed. His ever-present support for the last 22 years, and his willingness to be a guinea pig while I experimented with many of the training methods you will find in this book, contributed greatly to the final outcome.

INTRODUCTION

P SYCHIC ABILITIES are as much a natural part of every human being's potential as are the abilities to reason and analyze. Your physical senses and your psychic/spiritual senses are both quite human in nature. Once this fact has been accepted, the idea that psychic senses and abilities may be developed is no more strange than developing your physical senses and analytical ability. Not everyone does either to a great degree, but both *can* be done.

How, you may well ask, can I suggest that psychic abilities are part of human nature? I realize that it doesn't seem self-evident at first glance. It has been shown fairly convincingly by scientists from several different disciplines that humans are extremely complex beings. To start with, your physical body comes supplied with two very different types of nervous systems. The *autonomic* nervous system operates completely without the necessity of your conscious intervention to keep your blood flowing, your heart beating, your lungs working so that you can breathe, etc. The central and peripheral nervous systems, which combine to form the second type, normally require some conscious cooperation to accomplish tasks such as reaching out and picking up a book, driving a car, or throwing a ball. These two types of nervous systems are said to be the vehicles for two equally different types of "minds" known as the subconscious and conscious minds.

The subconscious mind is associated with the autonomic nervous system and the psychic/spiritual senses. The conscious mind is associated with the central and peripheral nervous systems and the physical senses. Reasoning and analytical abilities are functions of your conscious mind, whereas your instincts and psychic potential are functions of your subconscious mind.

Most people are well aware of the basic functioning of the conscious mind for obvious reasons. The objective faculties of seeing, hearing, tasting, smelling, and feeling associated with the conscious mind are things that most school children learn about in grammar school. In fact, such things are taken a bit too much for granted. How long has it been since you reminded yourself how your objective faculty of vision works? How long has it been since you *completely* observed your surroundings?

It is important to remember that all of your objective senses are designed to limit the amount of information that comes into your brain by way of the central and peripheral nervous systems. You only take in that subset of the available information that is necessary to interact *adequately* with the world around you. To illustrate this point, I ask you to try the following experiment:

Experiment 1:

1. Ask five people to look at a complex poster for a period of two minutes.

2. Remove the poster from sight and ask them to write down a description of what they saw.

3. Compare their descriptions.

You will undoubtedly get five different descriptions, and it is unlikely that any one description will contain all the details of the poster.

The objective sense of sight leaves lots of room for interpretation by your conscious mind and is limited not only by what your brain requires to make sense of the world around you, but also by the state of your physiology. If your objective sense of sight is distorted by malfunction (near-sightedness, far-sightedness, etc.), injury, drugs or alcohol, your perception of the world will likewise be distorted.

Also, most people are not aware of the functioning of the subconscious mind. As you noticed from performing the above experiment, there is quite a lot of information available that your objective/physical senses, and therefore the conscious mind, simply ignores. Ordinarily this is just fine, since you would be overwhelmed completely if you had to process all the stimuli that actually impinged on your physical senses at any given time and would be entirely unable to function in a satisfactory manner. The information is nonetheless out there. As it comes into your sphere of influence, it is taken in at the level of the subconscious mind. You can prove this to yourself if you have ever had the urge to pick up a phone before it rang, or found yourself opening the front door before a visitor had a chance to knock. Your purely objective/physical senses were not responsible for your behavior. However, the certainty you had that someone was calling for you (either by phone or in person) had to come from somewhere. That somewhere was your subconscious mind. It had access to information from the world around you that your conscious mind simply had not picked up.

Most people old enough to read this book have had experiences similar to the ones described above. Perhaps you have referred to these experiences as hunches or even coincidences. Whatever you have chosen to call them in the past, I would like you to keep an open mind about the following possibility:

Spontaneous psychic experiences are the result of information from the world around you, which you ordinarily would not notice. These experiences are created when this information crosses the boundaries between your subconscious and conscious minds.

If what I am suggesting is true (and I believe that it is), then developing your psychic potential simply requires finding some way to access this greater store of information—at will. This can be accomplished by developing a reliable communication link between your subconscious and conscious minds. A bit later I will share with you exercises designed to do just this including a couple that were passed on to me by Brian Standing Bear Wilkes, a Cherokee teacher and personal friend.

If you are wondering how a psychic is able to reliably retrieve information from the subconscious mind that is associated with the past or future or has happened or will happen at a great distance away from the present location of that psychic; then you are actually using a bit of both your rational and psychic abilities to predict the next topic I plan to cover—the problem of time and space.

Time and space are concepts that your conscious mind uses to help you make sense of the world around you. Time and space are not *things*; you certainly cannot see, hear, taste, feel, or smell them in any physical sense. Yet you objectify them by associating them continuously with material manifestations such as the duration of the light and dark parts of what you call a day, and how far you can walk, drive, etc. during parts of this day. You have also associated the duration of time with the extent of space.

Acting as if time and space are real things does make a certain amount of sense when you utilize the reasoning abilities of your conscious minds. It is useful to know that in your *waking consciousness* it takes a certain amount of time to travel a specific distance in a particular vehicle traveling at a specific speed when you are planning a trip. Why the emphasis on "waking consciousness?" Think about the last dream that you had in which you traveled any "distance." The whole trip, even if it covered what you think of as vast distances, probably only took a very few minutes.

The above is an example of one of the most significant differences between the conscious mind and its faculties and the subconscious mind and its faculties. The conscious mind is limited by Time and Space. It is also limited by the partial information it uses concerning the world around us. The subconscious mind is limited by none of this. This means that you are actually capable of accessing a greater amount of information and more reliable information through the faculties of your subconscious mind (the psychic senses) than you can obtain through the use of your physical senses alone. The trick, of course, is learning to consciously use your psychic senses as well as you can already use your physical senses. Then you should learn to improve your use of both types of senses. Once that is done, you can combine your psychic abilities and perceptions with your physical perceptions and abilities to analyze and reason in a balanced and sane manner. This process will eventually enable you to use the best of both of the minds you were born with.

I am writing this book to help you develop your psychic potential sanely. As you may have gathered from the last paragraph, this can only be accomplished if you develop your psychic skills in conjunction with the rest of your human potential (physical, mental, and spiritual). Therefore, I am going to structure the rest of this book as if it were a training manual designed to build up areas of your human potential that you may have ignored until recently.

Please read this book with the intent to practice and perfect the exercises as you go along. If you have questions concerning theories of the mind or the various levels of consciousness, please put them aside for the time being and work on the techniques. Once you have experienced the various lessons within this book, you are welcome to go back to theorizing. At that point you should be better qualified to do so. Should you have unresolved questions after working with all of the material in this book, please feel free to contact me through the publishers of this book.

The importance of practice and following the directions given cannot be stressed too much. There is a story that was told to me by Marti Mom Feather Kaelbli, a Cherokee elder and spiritual leader, that you will find instructive:

How The Bluebird Got His Color

At the time of Creation all the animals were the same grayish color. One day, a small bird landed on a tree above a beautiful pool of water. The water was such a lovely color that the little bird wished out loud that he could be that pretty color, as well. The pool heard the bird and said, "You can be blue, just like me." "How can I do that?" asked the bird. The pool told him that he must do exactly what he was told and then he, too, would be blue.

The pool said, "For the next three days you must wake up, dive into the water, and then fly back up to that tree branch and dry out completely. At the end of drying yourself for the third time you will be blue just like me." The little bird was so excited he could hardly wait for the next day. In the morning he dove into the water and flew back up to the tree branch and fluffed his feathers up so they would dry in the sun. Once he was dry he looked at first his right wing, then his left wing, and finally his body and found that they were all turning blue. The little bird was happy and so followed the pool's directions exactly for the next two days and indeed became the beautiful Bluebird that we know now.

Then Bluebird went off to show his friends his new color. Coyote saw him and asked him where he got his color? Bluebird told him about the pool and Coyote went off to the pool to find out how he could become blue. The pool told Coyote that if he followed exactly the directions he would be given, then he would be blue, too.

The pool gave Coyote the same directions he gave Bluebird except that Coyote was to dry himself off on the banks of the pool instead of sitting on a tree branch to do so. Coyote was so excited that he couldn't wait for the next morning, so he dove into the pool and climbed out and shook himself off. Then he looked at his four legs and body and saw that they were turning blue. He was so happy that he rolled around in the mud beside the pool and ran off to show his friends his new color.

Coyote first met Rabbit and said, "Look, look! I'm blue!" Rabbit said, "I don't think so." Then Coyote thought that Rabbit was just jealous and went on until he met Bear and said to him, "Look, look! I'm blue!" But Bear said, "I don't think that is the color you are." Coyote started to get nervous so he went off to find Owl. Owl was wise and would tell him the truth. When Coyote found Owl he said, "Look, look! I'm blue!" But, like the others, Owl disagreed and then told Coyote to look at himself carefully.

When Coyote did so, he found that he was a muddy shade of brown. He was very unhappy and went back to the pool and dove in to try and make himself blue, but it didn't work. When he asked the pool to help, the pool said that Coyote would have to be the color he was now since he hadn't followed his directions correctly. Then Coyote ran away to hide himself in the hills and to this day you can hear him cry on lonely nights, "I'm blue! I'm blue!"

Enough said! May you all be like Bluebird in your pursuit of psychic development!

CHAPTER 1

HOW TO DEVELOP
YOUR PSYCHIC ABILITIES

I SPENT A WONDERFUL weekend recently with a Cherokee elder and spiritual leader, who is now also my adoptive sister, Marti Mom Feather Kaelbli. Among other things, we discussed the writing of this book. Mom Feather said that she was taught that psychic abilities and spiritual experiences were just part of being human. "When the door moved without any flesh and blood being pushing it, we knew that a spirit was there and we greeted it." Mom Feather said she first met her guardian spirit when she was 4 years old. She immediately told her grandmother about the experience. Her grandmother then told Mom Feather that she had seen the spirit as well. In fact, Mom Feather's grandmother, Sally Brown (a Medicine Woman like her mother before her) had first seen that spirit when Mom Feather was only 18 months old.

Mom Feather and I grew up in very different environments. She was raised in the hills of Kentucky, while I spent my childhood in various upper middle class suburbs in Texas, Washington, DC, Indiana, Pennsylvania, and Connecticut. Regardless of these differences, we share the knowledge that what people call psychic abilities are just an ordinary aspect of our humanity.

In my case, I was fortunate enough to have parents who did not feel compelled to "correct" my perceptions, even though they were both highly educated. My mother was an elementary school teacher and my father is an orthopedic surgeon. They never talked me out of anything that I saw, heard, or felt. I was never told that something I perceived as real was "just my imagination." I seldom spoke to friends about what I now call psychic perceptions because, at the time, I just thought everyone experienced things the same way I did. Therefore neither friends nor acquaintances talked me out of this part of myself either. Later, when I left home for college, I was blessed with a martial arts teacher, Daniel K. Pai, Grandmaster of Pai Lum Kung Fu, who further encouraged my psychic and spiritual development. It was Daniel Pai who taught me how to learn and then how to teach people who were not as lucky as I was. They may have had friends that their parents couldn't see, but they were made to feel that these beings were not real. They may have had dreams that came true, but they were told it was just a coincidence. What a shame!

As you develop your psychic senses and gain spiritual experience you will begin to feel more whole. You will gain or perhaps regain a sense of wonder that you may have lost when you were a very young child. You will also gain access to the meaning of your own existence. This course of training will help you develop and use your psychic abilities so long as you persist in the practice of the exercises I will teach you. Before we begin, however, I would like to share with you the words of James O'Loughlin, a Cherokee/Shawnee Medicine Man.

During one of the first telephone conversations that my husband had with Jim O'Loughlin, Jim asked him: "Are you perfect?" Marty, naturally, answered: "No." At that point Jim said something that I believe is one of the sanest things anyone has ever said. He told Marty that of course he was perfect. Jim continued to explain that no matter what faults Marty thought he had, everything about him was perfect for the time, place, and circumstances he was in, and that he must remember that this is true of everyone. Whatever your current experience, level of ability, or circumstances in life, you are perfect just as you are for this particular time, place, and circumstance. Your decision to read this book and practice the exercises in it is also perfect. The path you have chosen will not be easy, but each step you take on it will be perfect. With this in mind, now we will begin.

The word "psychic" derives from the Greek word *psychikos* which means "of the soul" and the French word *psyche* which means "breath, life, soul." It is commonly used in modern English to refer to those things and forces which are outside the realm of known physical processes and to people who are sensitive to these things and forces. For the purposes of this book we will use the words "psychic faculties/senses," "psychic abilities," and "psychic experiences" to refer to those faculties/senses, abilities, and experiences that lie beyond the range of our physical senses and objective consciousness.

As I explained in the Introduction, psychic abilities are linked with the autonomic nervous system, instincts, and the subconscious mind. Developing the autonomic nervous system or your conscious awareness of it is key to accessing the information available to your psychic senses. This may require a bit of unlearning. Our conscious minds have learned to operate on a subset of the information which bombards the physical senses every second of our existence. Our five physical senses are not Nature's only means of conveying knowledge to us. There are sounds beyond the range of human hearing, produced by vibrations of either too high or too low a rate for our ears to pick up. Similarly, there are visual phenomena which our eyes cannot normally see. The same can be said of our three other physical senses. Therefore, our five physical senses do not transmit the existence of all things in the universe to our *conscious* minds. They are neither completely dependable nor completely reliable as transmitters of information.

Our conscious mind requires that the nerve impulses (sensory input) originating in the receptor cells of the peripheral nervous system be translated by the central nervous system and brain into thought forms recognizable by normal human consciousness. On the other hand, our subconscious mind recognizes and responds to information at a rather low level of organization. The psychic senses are linked to the subconscious mind and the autonomic nervous system. If we are to make input from the psychic senses accessible to the conscious mind, the information must be put in a form that the conscious mind can recognize and understand. Dreams that turn out to be prophetic and other spontaneous psychic experiences such as those mentioned in the Introduction prove that this process is possible.

To make conscious use of our psychic senses we develop our conscious awareness of our autonomic nervous system and work out a "language" understandable to both our subconscious and conscious minds. This is exactly how I will be going about the process of teaching you how to develop your psychic abilities.

Please begin by practicing the following exercises. They will both help you to relax your conscious mind and awaken consciousness within all parts of your body. As you work with these exercises, you may be surprised by how seldom you have paid attention to the life force within your physical body. You will also probably realize that the last time you did pay close attention was when some part of you malfunctioned. Take some time to think about this after you work with these first three exercises.

Exercise 1: Centering

1. Sit down in a comfortable but preferably straight-backed chair. Set your feet flat on the floor. Allow your hands to rest quietly in your lap.

2. Close your eyes and listen to the sound of your own heartbeat.

3. Begin to tune your breathing to the beating of your heart. Breathing in to a 4 beat, hold your breath in for a 4 beat, exhale to a 4 beat, and hold your breath out for a 4 beat. This is known as 4-fold breathing and should be done so that you breathe in and out through your nose while resting the tip of your tongue on the roof of your mouth slightly behind your front teeth.

4. Gradually slow your breathing down. Notice that your heart rate follows your breath now. Notice also that your thinking processes have begun to relax as well. Continue to slow your breathing down until you feel calm, relaxed, and develop a warm pleasant feeling in your belly. Once you achieve this experience, you will know what it feels like to be "centered."

Exercise 2: Grounding

1. Center yourself.

2. Forget about your heartbeat and place your attention on the soles of your feet. Allow a sensation of heat to build up under their arches.

3. Imagine now that a beam of golden light extends from the bottom of each of your feet.

4. Each time you exhale, imagine that these 2 beams of golden light extend further away from your feet and into the earth below you. (This may mean going through several floors and a building foundation first!) When your feet are firmly anchored in the earth, so that it seems it would be hard to move them if you tried, you will have experienced the feeling of being "grounded."

Exercises 1 and 2 should be practiced until you can center and ground yourself within a few seconds whether you are sitting, standing, or lying down (those beams of light can angle or curve down into the earth when necessary). You will be asked to center and ground yourself as a prelude to each of the exercises in this book. The primary reason for this is that these techniques help to alter your state of consciousness from that which your conscious mind uses on a daily basis. This change makes it more likely for you to access information from your subconscious mind. This same altered state is also useful in discouraging the interference of your conscious mind when you choose to keep it out of your way for a while.

Exercise 3: Awakening Awareness Within Your Physical Body

1. Sit in a comfortable chair or lie down on your bed.

2. Center and ground. You will soon be paying attention to individual body parts in turn. Maintain the rhythmic breathing that you started as you centered yourself and with each inhalation of your breath, lightly tense the body part mentioned and then with each exhalation of your breath, relax it.

3. Place your attention on the soles of your feet as if they were the only part of you. Try to feel your heels, the balls of your feet, and your toes.

4. Now move your awareness to your ankles. Pay attention to the bones and skin.

5. Next move your attention to your legs. Notice the feel of skin, bones, muscles, and blood vessels.

6. Now become conscious of the trunk of your body. Notice the pressure of your clothing against your skin. Pay attention to the internal organs in this area, moving from the abdomen up to the chest area. Be sure to listen to and feel the beating of your heart and the expansion and relaxation of your lungs.

7. Now move your awareness to your hands.

8. Next pay attention to your wrists.

9. Now focus on your arms, including elbows and shoulders.

10. Next move your consciousness to your lower face. Feel the teeth in your gums (no biting!).

11. Next pay attention to your ears.

12. Now be aware of your eyes.

13. Finally pay attention to the top of your head. Feel the hair growing on it and the brain working inside it.

14. Take a deep breath and slowly let it out while relaxing. Be aware of the feeling of energy circulating throughout your entire body. (If you have done the breathing and light tension, followed by relaxation as you were instructed in step two, you will feel a tingling sensation moving within the trunk of your body and through your arms and legs.)

NOTE: If you practice this exercise daily, giving about one minute's worth of attention to all body parts from the lowest extremity to the highest, you will not only awaken your conscious awareness of these parts and their functioning, but you will be vitalizing them as well. In addition, you will be forging the beginnings of a link between the autonomic nervous system and the conscious mind. At the very least you will feel physically invigorated, and at the most you will have started the process of tuning into the physical processes connected to your psychic potential.

If you wish to develop your psychic potential to its fullest, you will run into a number of paradoxical situations along the way. For instance, you will be told that you must build a link between your subconscious and conscious minds so that they can communicate clearly with one another, but you will also need to find ways to keep the faculties of your conscious mind (the physical senses and the abilities to reason and analyze) from interfering with the information that the psychic senses are trying to communicate to your conscious mind. Try the following exercise and you will see why this is so:

Exercise 4: Psychically Sensing Time

1. Make sure you have a watch or clock that keeps time accurately, but *don't* look at it before you begin.

2. Center and ground.

3. Ask yourself this question: "What is the correct time?"

4. Whether you "psychically" see, hear, or just know the answer, write it down in a small notebook that you should keep for this purpose. Be sure to record *only* your first impression.

5. Check the time on the watch or clock. Write down the correct time in your notebook. Compare the results.

6. Repeat steps 1–5 at irregular intervals until you can consistently intuit the correct time.

Do not become discouraged if it takes you a long time to perfect this skill. It is not unusual for those who try this exercise to intuit the correct time on the first try and then to fail miserably for the next 10–20 trials. Psychic impressions are subtle in nature. It is easy for us to allow our reasoning abilities to interfere with them. After being surprised by an initial success, you are likely to fall back on making "reasonable guesses" instead of waiting for a psychic impression. Only after giving up on these "guesses" will you once again pay attention to your psychic senses and intuit the correct time.

Now it would be wise if we added an exercise which is designed to develop both your physical and psychic senses simultaneously. The following exercise was given to me by Brian Standing Bear Wilkes:

Exercise 5: Learning to *See*

1. Find a place in the woods where you will be safe and undisturbed for up to one hour.

2. Sit comfortably on the ground with your back to a tree or large rock.

3. Open your eyes and look straight ahead.

4. Maintain this position, trying not to move any body part including your eyes.

5. Observe your environment.

6. When you can no longer remain still, end the exercise and contemplate your experience.

It is important to practice Exercise 5 until you can stay still and observe for roughly an hour at a time. It will generally be necessary to start with between five and fifteen minutes. Build yourself up to the full hour over the course of several sessions. The more immobile you are, the less of a threat you will be to both natural and supernatural creatures. Eventually they will come right up to you. As you practice this exercise, you will also start seeing things that your conscious mind tends to ignore under more ordinary circumstances. For instance, you may notice how particular blades of grass move or the actual progress of the wind as it moves individual leaves. You will learn to notice when you are using mostly your physical senses, mostly your psychic senses, or both types of senses equally. Even if you have a great deal of difficulty with this exercise, you will learn valuable things about yourself by asking such questions as: "Why can't I sit still for more than a few minutes?" or "What is it that keeps me from observing my surroundings in this manner?" This exercise should keep you busy for quite some time!

You now know that your psychic faculties are capable of accessing the information which is available to your subconscious mind. This includes everything that has been, is, and might be. You have been given exercises designed to develop your conscious awareness of your autonomic nervous system and exercises to alter your state of consciousness to one appropriate for consciously accessing information from your subconscious mind. You have also had some basic practice in learning the difference between the feel of a genuine psychic intuition and a logical guess. Now it is time to begin to work on learning a language which is understandable to both your subconscious and conscious minds.

How can we know what our subconscious minds can or cannot understand? Our best information comes from whatever experience we or others have had in the past by way of spontaneous psychic experiences. Prophetic dreams, flashes of foresight, feelings that something good or bad was about to happen, knowing who was going to call before the phone rang, concentrating hard on someone you needed to hear from and having them write, phone, or knock at your door, etc., are experiences most people have once in a while. Regardless of whether we psychically see, hear, feel or just know information which spontaneously crosses the boundary between our conscious and subconscious minds, the information most often comes across in symbolic form. Therefore, we can assume that our subconscious minds can understand symbols.

Our conscious minds certainly understand symbols. We consciously use a very complex symbol system every day when we speak or write our native tongue—English, for example. We use a numerical symbol system when we do arithmetic, higher mathematics, or plan a monthly budget. As we have proven with Exercise 4, where we practiced sensing time, our subconscious minds and their psychic faculties are capable of understanding simple questions. Specific information which is requested in our native language (such as, what is the correct time?) evokes an answer from our intuition. During the practice of that exercise, you then had the opportunity to find out how your subconscious mind communicated the desired information to your conscious mind. This was likely a rather subtle and simple flash of numbers, words, pictures, or even tactile impressions that told you what the correct time was. You may even have missed it a number of times before you realized where to place your attention.

Unless you are one of the few people who allowed their psychic and physical faculties to develop simultaneously from birth to adulthood, you probably have a conscious mind which can understand your native language at an adult level whereas your subconscious mind probably understands it at only a very basic (4-year old) level. It is possible that your subconscious mind may not be able to communicate with your conscious mind at even that degree of sophistication right now. If this is the case, then it makes a great deal of sense to teach both the conscious mind and the subconscious mind a symbolic language that they can learn to understand and use together. This should prove to be less frustrating in the long run.

Most of the "psychic sciences" and "reading methods" that have been developed over the ages provide useful symbolic languages for this purpose. Tarot cards are extremely useful since each card symbolizes a particular concept or set of concepts, and can be arranged in different positions in a card "layout" to communicate specific information. Numerology classifies concepts in a very organized fashion and can also be used quite effectively. I have found that the two together make a very complete package. I will be teaching you how to use them in the next few chapters.

CHAPTER 2

THE TAROT AS A SYMBOLIC LANGUAGE

TAROT CARDS ARE USED for a number of very practical purposes. They are designed to teach us how to balance our psychic/spiritual perceptions with our rational/logical/analytical thinking. This balanced use of our intuition and intellect helps us determine how to choose wisely between the options presented to us as we walk our individual paths in life. It helps us answer such questions as:

> For what career should we train?
> Whom should we seek to be our life partner?
> Where should we live?
> How should we deal with difficult times?

Efficient use of our intellect and intuition enables us to form a more complete perception of reality in all of its aspects by viewing it from different perspectives. This in turn helps us make wiser choices than if we relied only on one of these abilities.

Decks of tarot cards come in many shapes, sizes, and designs. They are easily obtained at most ordinary bookstores as well as New Age shops. I will be asking you to use a deck in the next set of psychic development exercises. Therefore, it would be advisable to obtain a deck or make one for yourself before reading further.

Tarot decks normally contain seventy-eight cards. Twenty-two of them are known as the Major Arcana. These are designed to embody the greater concepts and transitions that affect human lives. The other fifty-six are divided into four suits. These are normally the suits of Cups, Rods, Pentacles, and Swords. Some tarot decks label these suits a bit differently (calling Pentacles either Disks or Coins, etc.). These cards are called the Minor Arcana. They are designed to convey the smaller details of day-to-day living.

The most important aspect of choosing a tarot deck for yourself is to pick one whose style "speaks" to you. Take a look at the various kinds that are available. If you prefer a rather plain style and bright colors, the Rider-Waite deck will serve you well. If you prefer a plain style with muted or darker colors, the Morgan Greer deck should do. If you have a background in the Qabalah and Astrology and like a flamboyant style of artwork, the Thoth deck is a good choice. The Sacred Rose deck is beautiful and has a mystical flair to it. The Morgan Tarot is filled with 1960s craziness. For theater buffs, the Shakespearean Tarot should work rather nicely. There are decks that use Native American symbolism, ones that would appeal to lovers of science fiction, others that are designed with women in mind such as the Motherpeace deck, and there is even a Disney Tarot! As long as you believe you will be able to relate to the style in which your tarot deck is drawn, all will be well.

The tarot is especially effective in helping us to use symbols as doorways to a greater understanding of ourselves and our world. Each card is a symbol designed both to convey specific information and also to invite you to contemplation. In this way, the tarot's symbols help you to better understand yourself and your environment. This understanding in turn leads to the wisdom you will need to help yourself and others deal with life's complexities.

Once you have your tarot cards, take them out of their box and get familiar with them. Each deck normally is accompanied by a small booklet which gives you the basic meanings associated with the cards. These basic meanings will do as a starting point.

Have you ever watched a baby learn his/her first words? Do you remember how you were taught the alphabet and then how to read? If the answer to these two questions is yes, then you will have some idea about how to teach your conscious mind what the individual cards mean to you.

Exercise 6: Teaching Your *Conscious* Mind The Meanings of Individual Tarot Cards

1. Center and ground.

2. Sit in a chair in front of a desk or table in a well lighted room.

3. Look at each card and its title, then associate it in your mind (initially) with the basic meaning presented in the little booklet which came with your deck.

4. Stand up and replace the deck in its box.

5. Repeat at least once a day until you no longer need to look at the booklet to know what the basic meaning of each individual card is. (If you are a quick study, then do this exercise for at least seventy-eight days.)

As you practice the next exercise, you will see that teaching your subconscious mind the meaning of each card must be done in a slightly different manner.

Exercise 7: Teaching Your *Subconscious* Mind the Meanings of Individual Tarot Cards

1. Center and ground.

2. Sit in a comfortable chair in a dimly lighted room. The room should be quiet, and you should arrange things so that you will not be interrupted for 15–30 minutes.

3. Start with the first of the Major Arcana and use only one card per day. Set the card up so that you can see it clearly and note its title. Review briefly its basic meaning from the booklet which came with your deck.

4. Maintain the rhythmic breathing that you began in Step 1 and gaze at the card quietly until you feel as though you have completely absorbed its meaning for you on a deep level.

5. Stand up, turn up the lights and replace the card in your deck.

6. Repeat daily using a different card each day until you have been through all seventy-eight cards.

You can encourage the subconscious mind to interact with the conscious mind while learning the language of the Tarot by doing the following exercise.

Exercise 8: Integrating Subconscious and Conscious Meanings for Individual Tarot Cards

1. Center and ground.

2. Before you go to bed, choose one tarot card that you have already worked with in Exercises 6 and 7. Study its

basic meaning in your little booklet, and take a good look at it making sure to note its title just before you go to bed.

3. Ask yourself for further enlightenment concerning this card during the course of the night while you sleep.

4. Go to sleep knowing that whatever you need will be revealed.

5. When you wake up, take 5 minutes to center and ground, then let anything that you should know about the selected tarot card rise to the surface of your consciousness.

6. Record your impressions in a journal, even if you think nothing came through. The form on page 18 should be useful for this purpose.

Now I know you probably won't spend the next seventy-eight days and nights following the directions given in Exercises 6–8 to the letter. I have been working as a psychic and spiritual adviser for over twenty-five years, have worked with tarot cards for over thirty years, and have taught a great many students; so I really do know that 99 percent of you who read this book will practice the art of procrastination now that real work has become necessary. But don't give up! You can develop your psychic abilities even if you work on these exercises once in a while. It will just take longer.

In the light of these realities, I am going to give you yet another set of exercises. I expect that you may find them a bit more exciting since they involve doing actual psychic readings with your tarot cards. You can work with these exercises right now even if you haven't completed your seventy-eight day program with exercises 4–7 yet.

There are a few things I need to explain before I give you directions on how to do a tarot card reading. First, the seventy-eight cards that make up your tarot deck should be viewed as a kind of conceptual alphabet. Each card is a

Name _____ Date _____

Weather conditions _____

_____

Health _____

_____

Quality of concentration or your current ability to focus on the task at hand _____

_____

Tarot card _____

Deck used _____

Impressions and notes _____

_____

_____

_____

_____

_____

_____

pictogram. It embodies an idea. These pictograms can be put together just like words are put together to make sentences, and sentences are put together to make paragraphs. The structure that allows us to put the tarot cards together to gain the "full picture" in any reading is called a "spread." There are all kinds of different spreads that have been designed by tarot card readers. These spreads allow you to access all types of different information for yourself and others. The most common spread is called the Celtic Cross. It may, in fact, be outlined in the little booklet that came with your tarot deck.

Although it can be useful in certain kinds of situations (when clients have just one question or one problem they wish to address), I have found that the Celtic Cross is a rather limited structure. More often than not, someone who seeks out a psychic requires more detailed information than the Celtic Cross was designed to access. I have developed two spreads that will work for most people under most circumstances. They are the Current Trend Spread (see figure 1, page 20) and the Time Spread (see figure 2, page 21).

Exercise 9: Daily Reading for Yourself

(To be done at the beginning of your day.)

1. Center and ground while sitting in a chair in front of a table, dresser, or other clear surface.

2. You will be using the Time Spread so:

   • Assign each time period the length of two hours.

   • Ask yourself what your day will be like.

   • Shuffle the deck until you feel ready to begin the layout.

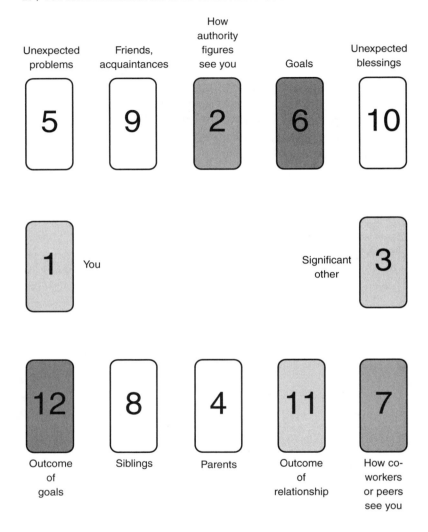

1. Lay out the cards in the order indicated by the numbers inside the card outlines.
2. Pay attention to the patterns suggested by the Relationship Cards ▯; Occupation Cards ▯; and Goal Setting Cards ▯.

Figure 1. The Current Trend Spread

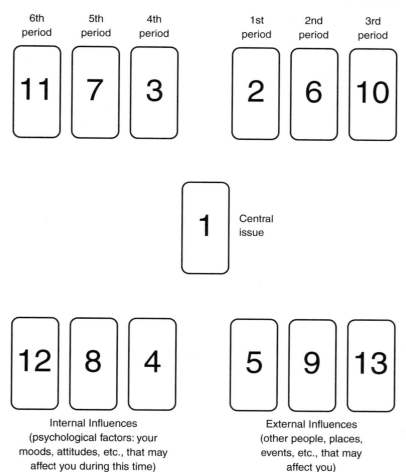

1. Lay out the cards in the order indicated by the numbers inside the card outlines.
2. When assigning time periods make sure they are all the same duration for any one reading. This should be decided before laying out the cards.
3. Time periods: assign a specific period (hours, days, weeks, etc.) to these top 6 cards.

Figure 2. The Time Spread

• Lay out the cards following the order indicated by the numbers inside the cards in Figure 2 on page 21.

• Briefly go over the meanings of the cards in the context of this spread.

• If you don't like what you see during any given two-hour period, check the psychological influences and see if anything concerning your attitude, mood, etc. might be the cause. If it is, then work on changing that problem so that the time period in question may be changed for the better. Remember that what hasn't happened doesn't need to happen! Always look for ways to change things for the better! If you don't think psychological factors are involved, check the outside influences and see if anything there might create a problem for you. If an outside influence is the cause of a potential problem, it may be a bit tricky to change or avoid, but usually something can be done.

• If you can't understand the reading very well, don't worry. Leave it out on a surface where it won't be disturbed.

• Come back and look at the reading twelve or more hours later (towards the end of your day).

• Now you are going to cheat big time! You know what happened during your day, so retrofit what happened into the six two-hour time periods. In other words, calibrate your experience with the six cards to better understand their meaning to you. In this way you will find out more about how your subconscious mind relates to the tarot cards as symbols and in the future you can take that into account when you do your readings.

Exercise 9 should be done daily. It will help your conscious and subconscious minds understand each other's symbols. It will also help you to gain some much-needed objectivity when you read for yourself. It is often said that you should-n't read tarot cards for yourself because you are likely to see either wish fulfillment or your worst fears rather than reality. This is because it is hard to keep your emotions in neutral for this type of reading. If you do Exercise 9 on a regular basis you will become so used to reading for your-self that you should be able to maintain your objectivity even in the most stressful of circumstances.

Now before I turn you loose to read for other people, you need to understand a couple of basic Do's and Don'ts.

DO

1. Ask the people you read for if they have any particular concerns or questions to which you should pay attention.

2. Use your subconscious faculties to *access* information.

3. Use your conscious faculties to *interpret* the information.

4. Take advantage of any courses on counseling that come your way, especially if you plan to read for strangers now or in the future.

DON'T

1. Don't be afraid to say: "I don't know," or "I could be wrong."

2. Don't leave the person that you have read for feeling as if there is no way to avoid or work on unresolved problems to produce a better result. Look to the reading for clues. Bad outcomes can be the result of bad attitudes, short-sighted-ness, over-reactions to outside influences, etc. If you can't think of anything to turn problems into opportunities, sug-gest counseling with appropriate mainstream professionals.

3. Don't diagnose health problems. It is OK to strongly suggest a trip to the doctor's office for a check-up, however.

4. Don't deliberately create self-fulfilling prophecies. Remember, you are providing a source of information for others and common-sense advice based on that information. You are *not* offering to run their lives for them.

With that out of the way, it is now time to enlist the help of all of your friends and family members so that you can get some practice reading tarot cards for others. Sometimes it is difficult to read for people you know well. This is because you are likely to have quite a number of preconceptions about the type of people they are, their hopes and fears, and what they really want out of life. However, when you begin to use the tarot for the benefit of others, it is always safer to start with those whom you are least likely to upset and/or those who will be willing to give you honest feedback. With luck, your friends and family members will fall into one or both of these categories.

Exercise 10: Reading Tarot Cards for Others

1. Sit down across a table or desk from the person for whom you plan to read tarot cards. (This person will now be known as your "client.")

2. Take a minute or two to make this person comfortable. Ask if there is anything your client wants you to focus on.

3. Center and ground (you should be able to do this quickly).

4. Deliberately tune your breathing to your client's as you begin to shuffle the cards.

5. When you are ready ask your client to cut the deck whatever number of times comes into your mind. Then have the person put the deck together any way he or she chooses.

6. Take the deck back and begin by laying out the Current Trend Spread.

7. Take your time to look at the whole spread and ask yourself what sticks out as the most important area of your client's life. (You may notice that the relationship cards are unusual, the career cards may seem odd in some way, or perhaps the goal setting cards catch your attention.)

8. Start with card #1. This represents whoever is getting the reading. Explain what the card means. Allow a brief quiet space for your subconscious mind to fill in any additional details and report them as you perceive them.

9. Move on to whatever area of your client's life caught your attention in step 7. Don't be afraid to put several cards together to come up with the information that your client needs. For instance, if card #7 shows that co-workers and/or peers view your client as a disruptive force, but authority figures see him or her as a conscientious worker, then your client may be working harder than those co-workers. This could be because your client's co-workers are lazy or because your client gets involved in work and regularly skips lunch and breaks and inadvertently makes co-workers look bad by comparison. *Use your psychic faculties to intuit information, use your analytical and reasoning abilities to interpret that information and give appropriate advice!*

10. Move on from the above to any other information that seems pertinent. Not all of the cards need to be examined during any given reading. After all, there will be some

issues you just don't need to go into. Let your intuition guide you concerning these matters.

11. When you feel as if you are finished, ask your client if he or she has any questions.

12. If there are questions, answer them to the best of your ability based on the spread. If you need further information allow your "client" to draw a card or two from what remains in the deck to access this information.

13. When you are done, put the cards away and go on about your daily business.

Do not be discouraged if your first readings sound elementary, a bit like your books from first grade. It takes time to become fluent in any language. With the tarot, you are not only teaching both your subconscious and conscious minds a new language, but you are constantly modifying your conscious mind's understanding of that language as your subconscious mind develops its own "dialect." *Practice, practice, and more practice makes perfect!*

CHAPTER 3

NUMEROLOGY AS A
SYMBOLIC LANGUAGE

N UMBERS, LIKE WORDS, are symbols. They represent the basic units of force which underlie all changes and progressions in the universe. You may already be in tune with the significance of certain numbers in your life. Do you have what you call a lucky number? Have you noticed that certain numbers show up again and again in your daily experiences? Do you ever have a feeling that a certain time is bad for you because of the numbers involved? If you have answered "yes" to any of the above questions, then your subconscious mind is already trying to use numbers to communicate with your conscious mind.

You can teach your conscious and subconscious minds the language of Numerology in much the same way that you taught your two minds the language of the tarot. The psychic science of Numerology works on the basis that all that is, has been, and might be within the universe can be symbolized by nine elemental numbers and the Master Numbers, 11 and 22. Some of the meanings associated with these numbers are listed in Table 1, pages 28–33.

As you can see from Table 1, the numbers 1–9 deal primarily with the ordinary abilities of humankind and our reaction/response to the universe of which we are integral parts. The numbers 11 and 22 are known as Master Numbers because they symbolize the highest potential that

Table 1. Meanings of Numbers

NUMBER	GOOD Characteristics	BAD Characteristics
1	The Self at its best, Original and creative ideas, Beginnings, Progressive ideas, Willpower, Self-assurance, Assertiveness, Decisiveness, Independence, Leadership, Courage	Egomania, Aggression, Arrogance, Bullying, Isolation, Inferiority complex, Indecision
NUMBER	GOOD Characteristics	BAD Characteristics
2	Putting other's needs before own, Nurturing, Understanding, Romance, Sensitivity, Diplomacy, Loyalty to a cause, Partnership and cooperation, Attention to details, Gestation, Sense of rhythm, Consideration for others	Neediness, Paranoia, Self-deception, Overly emotional, Shyness, Apathy, Peace at any cost, Slyness, Appeasement

(continued)

Table 1. Meanings of Numbers *(Continued)*

NUMBER	GOOD Characteristics	BAD Characteristics
3	Expression of the self, Social ambition, Communication skills, Charming, Outgoing, Performing arts, Appreciation of the beautiful, Enjoyment of life, Creative imagination, Personal style, Physical beauty	Show-off, Anti-social behavior, Mythomaniac (habitual liar or exaggerator), Superficial gossip, Jealousy, Scattering energies, Follower of fads, Tease, Personal conceit
NUMBER	GOOD Characteristics	BAD Characteristics
4	Practical, Disciplined, Good at physical work, Good physical and mental endurance, Systematic approach to challenges, Orderly and organized, Precision, Honest and reliable, Patriotic, Love of home, nature, and earth, Respectable	Too practical, Lack of personal discipline, All work, but no play, Defensive, Limited viewpoint, Too cautious, Stubborn, Envious of others, Violent, Crude, Ill-tempered

(continued)

Table 1. Meanings of Numbers *(Continued)*

NUMBER	GOOD Characteristics	BAD Characteristics
5	Personal freedom, Adaptable, thrives on change, Resourceful, trouble-shooter, Active, Adventurer, risk taker, Curiosity, loves surprises, Works well with groups, Sensual	Self-indulgence, Irresponsible, Impulsive, Restless, Addiction, Fickle, Overly critical of others
Number	GOOD Characteristics	BAD Characteristics
6	Responsible behavior towards others, Social awareness, Good mediation skills, Problem solver, Serving in a field of human service, Attention to the good of all, Balance, Truthfulness and justice, Good domestic skills, Good artistic sense, Persistence,	Irresponsible social behavior, Interfering in the affairs of others, Slavish behavior, Overly anxious, Domestic violence, Self-righteousness, Stubborn

(continued)

Table 1. Meanings of Numbers *(Continued)*

NUMBER	GOOD Characteristics	BAD Characteristics
7	Knowledge of self as part of the cosmic whole, Wisdom, Intelligence, Desire to explore the unknown, Desire to explore inner space, Desire to study all areas of knowledge, Written communication skills, Mysticism, Good powers of observation, Faith in the goodness of life, Good powers of deduction, Dignity, Refinement of taste, Perfected thinking	Ignorance of self as part of the cosmic whole, Closed-mindedness, Pessimism, Fear, Confusion and frustration, Depression, Dishonesty, Sarcasm, Escapism, Addiction

(continued)

Table 1. Meanings of Numbers *(Continued)*

NUMBER	GOOD Characteristics	BAD Characteristics
8	Freedom from material need, Good business sense, Success, Powerful, Good judgment, Executive ability, Responsible and fair authority figure, Ethical in business	Greed, Materialistic, Power madness, Cruelty, Abuse of authority, Poor judgment, Ruthlessness, Vindictive
NUMBER	GOOD Characteristics	BAD Characteristics
9	Selflessness, Giving of self, Completion, Understanding of the big picture, Unprejudiced (we are each other), Compassion for all people, Forgiveness, Generosity, Inspiring artist, Self-sacrifice, Romantic idealism, Fulfillment	Selfishness, Irresponsible, Emotional extremes, Extravagance, Vulgarity, Easily manipulated, Bitterness, Plays the blame game, Extreme waste

(continued)

Table 1. Meanings of Numbers *(Continued)*

NUMBER	GOOD Characteristics	BAD Characteristics
11	Idealism, Creative ability, Visionary ability, Intuition, Inventive and artistic genius, Spirituality, Ability to see all sides of a question, Powerful intellect,	Fanaticism, Lack of purpose, Wasted talent, Delusional, Egocentricity, Dishonesty, Abuse of the powers of the mind, Perversion,
Number	GOOD Characteristics	BAD Characteristics
22	Practical idealism, Practical genius, Mastering the material world, Philanthropy, Power on all levels, Highest service to mankind	Materialistic greed, Extreme power abused, Fascism, Crime, Indifference to the fate of mankind, Evil

humankind is capable of realizing and the lowest depths to which we are capable of sinking. The even numbers tend to symbolize somewhat more practical and occasionally more passive qualities, while the odd numbers represent our more intellectual, spiritual, and usually more active abilities.

Take some time to become familiar with the meanings associated with these numbers and then try the following exercises:

Exercise 11: Casting and Analyzing Your Birth Name Chart

1. Center and ground.

2. Sit at a table or desk in a well lit room. Be sure to have a pencil or pen and some paper available.

3. Take a piece of paper and print your full name (or the name of whomever you choose to do a chart for) as it was written on your (or his or her) birth certificate.

4. Use Table 2, page 34, to determine the correct number for every letter in your name. Then write the number under the letter in your name. (Jr., Sr., II's, etc., should not be included).

5. Add up the numbers that make up your birth name. If the total is more than 1 digit in length (unless the total is 11 or 22), you will add each of the digits together until you reduce it to a single digit. See the example below.

Table 2. Numerical Value of the Alphabet

1	2	3	4	5	6	7	8	9
A	B	C	D	E	F	G	H	I
J	K	L	M	N	O	P	Q	R
S	T	U	V	W	X	Y	Z	

```
J O H N   D O E
1 6 8 5   4 6 5
1 + 6 + 8 + 5 + 4 + 6 + 5 = 35 = 3 + 5 = 8
```

This number symbolizes your *natural abilities*, those abilities that you were born with (or brought with you from past lives if you believe in reincarnation).

6. Add up and reduce the numbers that are associated with the **vowels** of your birth name in just the same way. (If a "Y" or "W" acts as a vowel, then treat it like one.) This number represents what initially motivates your actions in this life.

```
J O H N   D O E
  6         6 5
6 + 6 + 5 = 17 = 1 + 7 = 8
```

7. Now do the same with the **consonants** in your birth-name. The result symbolizes your beginning "bigger than life" dreams, **your impression of what you could be** in this lifetime.

```
J O H N   D O E
1   8 5   4
1 + 8 + 5 + 4 = 18 = 1 + 8 = 9
```

8. Write down the numbers 1–9 and place each of the letters of your birth name under the appropriate number.

```
1  2  3  4  5  6  7  8  9
J        D  N  O     H
            E  O
```

9. Write down the numbers that have no letters under them. These numbers indicate the lessons that you must learn before you reach the end of your first Major Cycle in life. (The first Major Cycle ends between the ages of 27 and 35. More on this later.)

The Karmic Lesson Numbers for John Doe are 2, 3, 7, and 9.

Now count these numbers (2, 3, 7, 9 = 4 numbers) and subtract the result from 9 (9 − 4 = 5). This number represents how you will initially respond to crisis situations.

The Subconscious Response to a Crisis Number for John Doe is 5.

10. Finally notice which numbers have the most letters under them. These numbers represent things you may have learned so well in past lives that you may take them too much for granted this time around.

5 and 6 are these numbers for John Doe.

11. Center and ground once again and look at the information you have discovered. Ask your subconscious mind which number or set of numbers is most important to look at first. Check it out and interpret it in light of its context. For instance if you notice that the natural abilities and beginning motivation numbers for John Doe are the same, what does this mean to you? Proceed from this beginning until you have come to understand John Doe through his chart. Remember that people do learn new things which

modify their motivations over time. This will mean that the birth name chart is most useful while someone is still building the foundation for what he or she is going to do in life.

12. Put your paper and analysis in a file marked, "Birth Name Charts" and keep it in a safe place.

Note: You should try your hand at as many charts as you can. Always ask for feedback from your clients. This will help you understand how to work with the numbers in different contexts. (Remember, if you get an 11 or 22, do not reduce any further.)

Exercise 12: Casting and Analyzing a Birthdate Chart

1. Center and ground.

2. Sit at a table or desk in a well lit room. Be sure to have a pencil or pen and some paper available.

3. Write down your birthdate (or that of someone else) in numerical form on a piece of paper. See the example below.

April 4, 1930
4 - 4 - 1930

4. Add and reduce the digits in this birthdate just as you did with the birth name chart in Exercise 10.

April 4, 1930
$4 + 4 + 1 + 9 + 3 + 0 = 21 = 2 + 1 = 3$

This number represents the **Destiny** towards which you (or your client) can work.

5. Now note the following formulas:

A = Birth Month
B = Birth Day
C = Birth Year

6. Now use the following birthdate chart to determine the appropriate information about the birthdate we are working with (April 4, 1930).

MAJOR CYCLES	PINNACLES	CHALLENGES
1 = A	1 = A + B = D	1 = A – B = H
2 = B	2 = B + C = E	2 = B – C = I
	3 = D + E = F	
3 = C	4 = A + C = G	3 = H – I = J

Explanation of Terms Found in a Birthdate Chart

In Numerology there are three Major Cycles. The first Major Cycle is the time during which you build the foundation for your life through "growing up," learning, and maturation. The second Major Cycle is the time during which you build a family and career upon your foundation. The third Major Cycle is the time when you fulfill your destiny if you choose to do so.

The Pinnacle periods in Numerology represent times when a particular course of action works best in your life. That course of action is related to the Pinnacle number.

The Challenges shown on a Numerological Birthdate Chart indicate the types of obstacles that will face you. They might also be said to indicate those things that will make you stronger if you deal with them in a constructive manner.

MAJOR CYCLES	PINNACLES	CHALLENGES
1 = 4	1 = 4 + 4 = 8	1 = 4 − 4 = 0*
2 = 4	2 = 4 + 4 = 8	2 = 4 − 4 = 0*
	3 = 8 + 8 = 16 = 1 + 6 = 7	
3 = 1 + 9 + 3 + 0 = 13 = 1 + 3 = 4	4 = 4 + 4 = 8	3 = 0 − 0 = 0*

*Note: If the result is a negative number just ignore the minus sign.

The first Major Cycle builds the foundation for who you are going to be and what you are going to do "when you grow up." It lasts from Birth until the age determined by subtracting your Destiny number from 36. In other words, the first Major Cycle may be as short as 27 years or as long as 35 years: 27 years old for those with 9 Destinies, and 35 years old for those who have 1 Destinies. The first Pinnacle period lasts exactly as long as the first Major Cycle and represents your best mode of operation during this time. The first Challenge lasts from Birth until Death.

The second Major Cycle represents a family and career orientation and lasts until roughly 54 years of age. The second through fourth Pinnacle periods represent your best mode of operation for consecutive 9 year periods starting after the end of the first Pinnacle period. The third Major Cycle represents the time period in which you will fulfill your Destiny if you choose to do so. The second and third Challenges last from the beginning of the second Major Cycle of your life until Death. See below for how this would work out for the birthdate of April 4, 1930.

MAJOR CYCLES	PINNACLES	CHALLENGES
1 = 4 (Birth–1963)	1 = 8 (Birth–1963)	1 = 0** (Birth–Death)
(1961–1966 Major Transition)***	(1991–1999)****	
2 = 4 (1964–1985)	2 = 8 (1964–1972)	2 = 0 (1964–Death)
(1983–1988 Major Transition)	3 = 7 (1973–1981)	
3 = 4 (1986–Death)*	4 = 8 (1982–1990)	3 = 0 (1964–Death)

*Major Cycles must start on a "1" or "5" Personal Year. Personal Years are found by adding your birth day number to your birth month number to the year number in question. For the chart above, 4 + 4 + 1 + 9 + 8 + 6 = 32 = 3 + 2 = 5. This is the year closest to age 54 that the third Major Cycle could start on.

**When a 0 Challenge exists, this indicates that the person is an old soul who must take on a great deal more responsibility than the average person would. He or she will be responsible in some way for the growth of others as well as his/her own growth (physically, mentally, and spiritually).

***Two years before and after the beginning of a new Major Cycle represents a transition period during which all hell seems to break loose as people try to adapt to the new circumstances of their lives. These years often bring difficulties with personal relationships, job changes, moves, and the like.

****If the person is still alive after 1990 he or she will change Pinnacle periods in 1991. The Pinnacles are then reused in order for the next nine years.

7. Center and ground once again and look at the information you have discovered. Ask your subconscious mind which number or set of numbers is most important to look at first. Check it out and interpret it in light of its context.

8. Get up and put your paper and analysis in a file marked, "Birthdate Charts" and put it in a safe place.

Note: You should try your hand at as many charts as you can. Always ask for feedback from your clients. This will help you understand how to work with the numbers in different contexts. (Remember, if you get an 11 or 22 do not reduce any further.)

In Numerology, context is everything. The number 1 as your Destiny number indicates that you will be a leader (if you choose to follow through with your Destiny) in whatever area of work you finally settle down to. It will take at least 35 years (the approximate length of your first Major Cycle) to get enough breadth and depth of experience to begin to make the best use of your abilities in the world. This Destiny also ensures that there will be no door with your name on it that says "Chief in Charge of Everything." With a 1 Destiny, you must create that door for yourself. If 1 is your first Major Cycle number, this indicates a time of needing to go it alone, learning to be independent and self-sufficient. A 1 as a second Major Cycle number indicates a time when there will be many opportunities for developing and using your leadership potential. A 1 as a third Major Cycle number indicates that the person involved will get a chance to start a new life in an independent manner. A 1 as a Pinnacle number gives you a greater degree of success in life if you take every opportunity to exercise your leadership abilities. A 1 as a Challenge number indicates that other people are likely to try to run your life and you need to learn the courage of self-determination.

Always allow your intuition to pick out the patterns and particular numbers that are most appropriate to deal with at any given time. Numerology is a very balanced psychic science. You will need to use both your intellect and your intuition to make the most of what it has to offer you.

Please note that it will take you quite a while to become really fluent in this language of numbers. It will be helpful if you repeat exercises 11 and 12 for yourself once a month. You can then compare your initial analysis with each subsequent one. In this way you will gain additional personal insight as you become better acquainted with this symbolic language known as Numerology. I also recommend, *The Secret of Numbers*, by V. Johnson and T. Wommack (see bibliography) to further explore Numerology.

CHAPTER 4

PSYCHIC ABILITIES VERSUS SPIRITUAL POWER

H UMAN BEINGS HAVE both physical and non-physical "bodies" which interpenetrate and support each other in order to provide a vehicle for our true Selves or Souls as they manifest and learn from this world of ours. Psychic abilities are standard equipment within these "vehicles." Other standard equipment which is provided for the use of our Souls in their earthly incarnations includes our intellects/minds, instincts, and basic physical senses.

All such abilities have their uses and their limitations. As we have seen, our physical senses are limited by time, space, their normal or abnormal range of operation, as well as the accuracy of our interpretations of that fraction of information from the world around us that our physical senses allow into our conscious minds. Our psychic senses are *not* limited by time, space, or fractional access to information. However, what we make of the information which we glean from our psychic senses *is* limited by the degree of accuracy with which we interpret that information for ourselves or others.

Psychic abilities should not be confused with spiritual power. It is quite possible to be psychically strong, yet spiritually weak. Our true Selves or Souls incarnate in this world to develop, learn, and grow towards the beings we were designed by Divinity to become. Since part of being human is to embody both animal and spiritual natures, we can choose to evolve spiritually through our earthly experience, merely focus on material desires, or do a little of both.

Psychic abilities are part of our animal nature in just the same way that our mental and physical abilities are. Therefore, our psychic abilities should become the servant of our true Selves, never the master. One of the best ways of ensuring this ideal situation is to develop a strong personal working relationship with the Divine by whatever name(s) you know it. If you can honestly offer all of your abilities (psychic and otherwise) to the god(s) of your heart on a daily basis, you will have gone a long way towards maintaining your sanity and developing your spiritual worth.

It is all too easy to forget that your natural abilities are gifts from That Which Created You. Certainly if you take the time to develop a physical or psychic ability to a high degree of proficiency, you should take some pride in that accomplishment. What you should not do is become "a legend in your own mind" who uses that ability merely to appear superior to others.

Psychic development without spiritual balance leads to the type of life style that makes you a menace to yourself and others. The desire to escape the ordinary trials and tribulations of life through the development of psychic abilities can be a sign of trouble. It has been my experience that the many religious sects, cults, and New Age groups that advertise techniques designed to promote this type of escapism along with a "feeling" of personal power do more harm than good. After all, most people really do have to live "in the world." Supposedly empowering experiences that have adverse overall effects on your character, behavior, or functionality should be evaluated accordingly. Some things truly can be judged by their fruits!

So how can we develop sufficient spiritual power to ensure that we use our psychic abilities in a sane and balanced manner? One of the easiest ways is to work within a spiritual community which promotes this type of growth.

Most religions (orthodox and alternative) support such activities as retreats and meditation. (The names given to these activities may differ depending on the religion involved. Don't let mere semantics get in your way.) It is usually necessary to ask about these practices unless you are already on course to becoming a priest(ess), minister, rabbi, etc. If you do not belong to one of these groups and do not choose to do so in the future, then you may find the going a bit rougher.

The basic techniques involved for developing a close working relationship with the Divine are fairly simple. Having the discipline to practice them on a regular basis is the hard part.

We are designed to live in the midst of both matter and spirit. All of our activities by their very nature can be both secular and spiritual simultaneously. The trick is knowing how to manifest them as both in our daily lives. This is not at all a simple matter. In fact, I suggest that in the beginning it will be easier to separate (as much as possible) the secular and spiritual aspects of your daily routine. Most religious traditions would agree. There should be a time for physical and mental work, a time for family and friends (emotional exercise), and a time for spiritual work during the course of your daily life. The proportion of the day that is devoted to these activities will vary greatly from individual to individual.

If you wish to develop the strong personal relationship with Divinity which will empower you spiritually, at least a tenth of your day should be devoted to spiritual work. This 2.4 hours could be spread out over the course of your day to include morning, midday, evening, and nightly devotions, exercises, and study. This time could also be collapsed into one or two longer periods of daily spiritual work. The rest of your day might be broken up into 9.6 hours which should be set aside for eating, sleeping, and physical exercise; 8 hours reserved for mental exertion (school, jobs, etc.); and 4 hours devoted to time spent with friends and family. This is merely a suggested schedule. You will have to assess your own lifestyle and needs before you will be able to discipline yourself with a schedule of any type. The important thing is to order your life. Only then will it be possible to establish a feeling for the meaning behind each aspect of it. Of course, you must also remain flexible enough to accommodate whatever changes become necessary due to unforeseen circumstances. Once you can appreciate the secular and spiritual aspects of your life individually, you can then begin to integrate the two.

There is another thing you must understand if you choose to seek an intimate relationship with Divinity on your own. First of all, you simply cannot expect the support of society. While it is true that most people do not deny the existence of Divinity, they behave as if contact (personal or otherwise) is unnecessary to their way of life. Contemplation, meditation, and prayer are viewed by many as very nearly a waste of time. Even some religious communities will fail to be particularly optimistic about the chances of finding "God" on your own. After all, they are in the business of providing "go-betweens" for the masses of people who do not choose to seek out a personal relationship with the Divine Source of their existence.

The point is that if you choose to work on your spiritual development in a solitary fashion, you cannot expect a great deal of public support for your efforts. In fact, you may have to endure a fair amount of ostracism by "ordinary" people, and worse yet, the acclaim of genuine "crazies." The only way to avoid some of this is to heed the directive given to mystics and magicians of all Ages: *be silent* about your quest unless you are among like-minded people.

Another hurdle you may encounter is that there are hardly any schools or training programs designed to help you on your way. However, you can gain the knowledge and skills required by learning techniques used by those who have walked this path before you. Many have recorded their experiences in writing. Some of these documents are still used in training seminarians. Below you will find an example of one of the methods used by Native Americans. It was explained to me by the Cherokee teacher, Brian Standing Bear Wilkes.

The *Vision Quest* is a standard religious practice among many Native American peoples. Visions were sought to provide guidance from the Creator concerning the life one was expected to lead. For example, the Vision Quest was used as part of the rites of passage into adulthood for males among the Lenape. Adolescent males were prepared to spend up to twelve days on this Vision Quest (neither eating nor drinking during that time). This rite was taken very seriously. In fact, if a young man failed to have a vision by the end of the twelfth day, it was deemed that he had learned nothing from his life up to that point! In consequence that young man would be given an herbal "remedy" which created delirium and seizures that wiped his memory clean so that he could start life over again. He was essentially reborn as an adult and needed to be taught how to live from the beginning.

After the Indian Removal Act in the 1830s, many Native American religious practices were outlawed. This problem made it necessary for Native Americans to adapt to the pressures of the time by modifying their behavior in such a way as to avoid notice by the authorities. Thus the Vision Quest which originally simply took as long as it took became a one- or two-day experience for some people. The version presented here is designed to take 1–4 hours. Its purpose is to tune up the sensitivity of all of your senses (physical and psychic). It is a good preparation for longer quests to communicate with the Creator and the Helping Spirits.

Exercise 13: Accelerated Vision Quest (Two People Required)

(It is a good idea to have worked on Exercise 5 on page 9 before attempting Exercise 13)

Preparation

1. The sponsor of this Vision Quest is responsible for doing everything. The quester simply needs to experience.

2. The sponsor must prepare a questing site in the woods which is secluded and relatively safe. The sponsor should clear the ground at the site and lay down a quilt or blanket next to a sturdy tree.

3. The sponsor must also prepare an observation site from which to observe the quester without intruding upon the experience.

4. A staging site or base camp must be prepared from which the quester begins and ends the quest.

5. The quester must abstain from food and water during this quest.

6. The quester should wear as little clothing as possible.

The Quest

1. At the staging site, the sponsor blindfolds the quester.

2. The sponsor then leads the quester to the questing site by a roundabout route.

3. The sponsor settles the quester on the blanket with his or her back to the tree. The sponsor removes the quester's

shoes. The quester may move about the questing site or simply stay put. The quester's job is to receive sensory input from the environment while surrounded by living organisms, all of which communicate with each other and may communicate with the quester. According to the Cherokee/Shawnee Medicine Man, James O'Loughlin, human beings are the only beings who have the ability to voluntarily change the frequency they communicate on. Therefore the quester should essentially "channel surf" to hear the inhabitants (natural and supernatural) of the site and learn as much as possible.

4. The sponsor withdraws to the observation site and keeps an eye (physical & psychic) on the quester. The sponsor must be prepared to rescue the quester should trouble result.

5. After ideally 4 hours, the sponsor will come to collect the quester and clean up the questing site.

6. The quester is then led back to the staging site by another roundabout route. (The sponsor should allow the quester to put on his/her shoes for this return trip.)

7. The sponsor removes the quester's blindfold and lets the quester talk about the experience. The sponsor should just listen. No interpretation from the sponsor should be forthcoming at this point.

Surprise

The quester is now told to go find the questing site. The sounds, smells, and other sensations of the previous 4 hours should call to the quester. Even if all the quester does is notice the effect his or her presence has had on a particular environment, the exercise will have succeeded. If the quester doesn't find the spot in an hour, then both the sponsor and the quester need to contemplate the problem for further enlightenment.

You will undoubtedly have to depend mostly on yourself for your initial training. This can be dangerous. Contact with Divinity is likely to shake up your comfortable and familiar world fairly drastically. At this point it might be wise to ask yourself if you have the objectivity and persistence to withstand the inevitable pressure to which you will be subjected.

One of the most difficult paradoxes you will face during the first stages of your training is the confusion created by the simultaneous requirements of developing enormous self-confidence and maintaining the virtue known as humility. The word humility derives from the Latin word *humus* which means earth. Being grounded in the truth is essential to your quest. The inward journey "Godward" is filled with illusions (most of our own making). Without a firm anchor in the truth, your quest may lead only to self-destruction.

Distractions are dangerous to those who decide to approach a relationship with Divinity on their own. The way is narrow across the abyss which separates the merely human from the supremely Divine and a fall is likely to be debilitating. However, all of us are called to this way at some time during our various lifetimes. The old saying, "many are called, but few are chosen" might be more accurately stated as "all are called, but few at any given time have the perseverance to stay the course." The sacred journey is essential to our spiritual survival, but it is far better to leave it for the future than to risk a premature beginning.

Almost anything or anyone can be a distraction. The most powerful distractions, however, are the ones that play on our egos, such as the desire for power or prestige. The ego gives rise to powerful forces which serve to test our endurance. The temptation of power is self-evident. The trap of self-delusion goes hand and hand with it and the second source of distraction, the desire for prestige. As we noted earlier, those who walk this path alone cannot expect the encouragement or acclaim of most other humans. Yet that is often what we crave, is it not? It is far more comfortable to lay the responsibility on others for determining our true worth than it is to face the naked truth about ourselves. But that is what you must do, in order to reach this particular goal.

Once you have made the decision to leave the relative safety of the masses and transcend their religions, you must first learn to trust the inner guidance that will lead you to Divinity. The gods did not stop speaking 2000 years ago, though in truth many of us have forgotten how to listen. The first step towards this goal requires a commitment to the type of daily living schedule that I spoke of earlier. Setting aside a dedicated period of time for physical, mental, emotional, and spiritual exercise will allow you to sort out the stimuli to which you are responding. For instance, if you are focusing on the physical requirements of your existence, you should be able to recognize the cues your body gives you concerning its needs. The same is true of all other aspects of yourself.

The next step is to keep a journal of daily events, feelings, and observations. This will help you to keep track of your progress. You may wish to use the journal form on page 52.

Although it would be nice to make your journal recordings close to the time the cause of the entry was experienced, it will not always be possible to do so. At least try to jot down a couple of notes to yourself which can be transferred to your journal later in the day.

Many spiritual traditions have tried to regulate the spiritual devotions of their adherents. As was stated earlier, establishing order in your life is the most important thing. One method designed to regulate one's spiritual exercises which I have found useful was suggested to me by William G. Gray. (He published a version of this in his *Western Inner*

Name _____ Date _____ Time _____

Hour was dedicated to _____

_____

Weather conditions _____

_____

Personal emotional/mental/physical state _____

_____

Description of event/observation/feeling _____

_____

_____

_____

_____

_____

_____

_____

_____

_____

Workings, pages xiv–xv.) The idea was to split up the time which you plan to devote to spiritual work into four distinct segments:

1. *Morning Meditation*: Take 5–10 minutes after you get up in the morning to concentrate on whatever spiritual studies you undertook the night before and allow any new information that may have come to you during your sleep to surface from the depths of your consciousness. Make your journal entry concerning this.

2. *Midday Invocation*: Take time during the middle of the busiest part of your day to intensely invoke the Inner Power you hope is trying to guide you towards your best pathway to enlightenment.

3. *Evening Study*: Use the bulk of your time for reading and study of spiritually relevant topics.

4. *Nightly Quest*: Choose a topic to "sleep on" just before going to sleep. This is done so that your deeper awareness, more active during sleep, may specifically deal with your needs.

After a month or two of following this schedule of spiritual exercises, you should begin to be able to recognize the proddings that arise from your deepest levels of awareness as they surface throughout the day. You will note that these proddings may not always arrive at a convenient time, however it is always wise to pay close attention to them. You should also note that indeed this inner guidance has always been available to you. In learning how to listen to it, you have taken a big step forward towards communicating with Divinity.

Patience will be important even after many years of experience with your Source of Inner Guidance. Even after you are confident that this communication can and does occur, it will not always be as plentiful or as comfortable as you might wish. There will be times when you will wonder if you are actually getting anywhere at all. There will also be times when you will feel overwhelmed by the direction in which you are being guided. Often as not, these times will coincide with inner proddings that demand your attention at all hours of the day and night when you really would rather be doing something a bit more frivolous—like eating or sleeping for instance!

If you find this as frustrating as most of us do from time to time, remember that communication is a two-way street. There is no reason in the world that you should not express the frustrations and difficulties you are having to the appropriate Source. After you ventilate your feelings, however, you should be prepared to faithfully go on about your daily business. Other people depend on you, and for their sakes you must continue on as usual even under the most trying of spiritual "black outs." Sooner or later (if you continue with your spiritual exercises and don't give up) something will happen to restore your confidence in your Divine guidance and Divinity itself, and you will have survived the single most difficult distraction of all—the dark night of the soul.

Once you have established a good working relationship with the god(s) of your heart, you will find that your psychic abilities will be a bit more dependable. Of course, you will still have to be careful to acknowledge the difference between that which you perceive psychically and that which is a direct communication from the Divine. The subject matter of the next chapter will help you sort this out as you learn the difference between psychic readings and *divination*.

CHAPTER 5

HOW PSYCHIC READINGS
DIFFER FROM DIVINATION

A S WE SAW IN THE last chapter, psychic abilities are part of the standard equipment that comes along with our physical bodies. These abilities may be nurtured and honed to a very great degree through disciplined exercise and constant use. Methods for doing so have been defined in chapters 1–3 of this book. As a good psychic, you must not only have the ability to access information through the psychic senses, you must also develop the ability to interpret this information correctly. Therefore the use of psychic abilities to do a psychic reading or interpret a psychic impression is still very much open to human error.

Divination is quite a different kettle of fish. All methods of divination are designed to find out what the will of Divinity is in a particular situation. In fact, some religious groups believe that discerning the will of God (or the gods) can be done by a religious practitioner who has little or no psychic ability. Most Christian churches would call the use of this ability an exercise of charism.

Oddly enough, most of the methods that psychics use to focus their abilities can also be used as divinatory tools. The tarot cards can be used to do either psychic readings or divinations. The main difference is in the mind and intention of the practitioner.

For instance, if you asked me to give you a brief synopsis of what was going on in your life right now and what to anticipate coming into it over the next six months, I would use the tarot cards to do a psychic reading for you. This type of information can be accessed by anyone who has developed both their psychic potential and their intellectual powers of reasoning and analysis. So in this case there is no need to bother God (or the gods) with something that human abilities are quite sufficient to handle. However, if you had experienced a vision or feeling that suggested you were required by Divinity to work with a particular person, go into a specific vocation, or even pursue a relationship with someone and were unsure whether this was indeed Divine prompting or your imagination, I would use tarot cards to perform a divination.

Divination requires that you allow the will of the god(s) of your heart to work through you. Therefore, most practitioners will take some time to prepare themselves before attempting to divine the answer to anyone's dilemma. Those of us who use the same type of tools (tarot cards, for instance) to focus our psychic abilities and to work divinations usually keep a special set which is consecrated to the god(s) of our heart for the purpose of divination, and a mundane set to use during the ordinary exercise of our psychic potential. Below you will find one method of consecrating a tarot deck which is to be reserved for the practice of divination.

Exercise 14: Consecrating a Tarot Deck (or any tool) for the Purpose of Divination

1. Select a new tarot deck which from the first will be used only for the purpose of divining the will of the Divine.

2. Prepare an area which at least for a time will be consecrated as a sacred place in which humans and god(s) may meet and communicate.

• Clean this area of all ordinary dirt.

• Use blessed salt-water to cleanse the area of anything that is unnecessary, unwanted, or just plain opposed to the purpose to which the space is being put.

Salt: [Hold dish with salt in it in your left hand and extend the palm of your right hand over it while saying] **As this salt can preserve things in the material world from corruption, so let it be the physical symbol of that which can preserve us from evil and corruption in the spiritual world.** [Make the sign of the Cosmic Cross while saying] **In the Name of the Wisdom** [with right hand touch forehead] **and of the Love** [touch heart] **and of the Justice** [touch right shoulder] **and of the Infinite Mercy** [touch left shoulder] **of the One Eternal Spirit.** [circle face] **Amen.** [with fingers of right hand touch under nose]

Salt in Water: [Sprinkle salt in small vessel of water with right hand, then hold vessel in left hand while extending your right palm over the water while saying] **As this blessed salt dissolves in water, may the two become an intentional agent for cleansing our bodies, minds, and souls as well as this space of all corruption and evil.** [Make the sign of the Cosmic Cross] **In the Name of the Wisdom** [touch forehead] **and of the Love** [touch heart] **and of the Justice** [touch right shoulder] **and of the Infinite Mercy** [touch left shoulder] **of the One Eternal Spirit.** [circle face] **Amen.** [touch under nose] [Dip the fingers of your right hand into the blessed salt-water and sprinkle it on yourself. Then take it to the east of your space and walk in a clockwise circle around the space sprinkling it and everything in it with the blessed salt-water.]

• Use blessed incense to seal the area to its intended purpose.

Light incense of sandalwood or frankincense and myrrh. Use stick incense or charcoal with powdered incense or oil on top of it. Hold the stick or burner in your left hand while extending your right palm over the smoke while saying: **May these elements of fire and air be blessed with the ability to seal ourselves and this space to our sacred service.** [Make the sign of the Cosmic Cross while saying] **In the Name of the Wisdom** [with right hand touch forehead] **and of the Love** [touch heart] **and of the Justice** [touch right shoulder] **and of the Infinite Mercy** [touch left shoulder] **of the One Eternal Spirit.** [circle face] **Amen.** [touch under nose]

• Cense yourself and the area while dedicating all to the intended purpose. Now go to the east and walk clockwise around the intended sacred space censing everything within it while consciously sealing it to your intended purpose.

3. Consecrate the tarot card to the god(s) of your heart

• Sprinkle the tarot deck lightly with the blessed salt-water while intending to cleanse it of everything which is unwanted, unnecessary, or just plain opposed to your intended use for it.

• Pass the tarot deck through the blessed incense smoke while mentally sealing it to your intended purpose.

• Invoke the blessing of Divinity upon yourself and the deck. Go to the west of your sacred space while holding your tarot deck in both hands and say:

Thou Great Invisibles whom I approach with reverence through the Western Gateway of the Inner World, connect thy consciousness to mine in communion with this tarot deck, and let us meet each other in the Way of Wisdom through the medium of Love.

Here on Earth, my hands and heart are opened before Heaven. Fill them with fervent and unfailing faith in the Divine compassion which encompasses my being.

Imbue this tarot deck with all that is needed so that when I work with it in the service of my fellow human beings and Divinity, the will of the Divine may be perceptible to me.

The will Divine be done in me, now and forevermore. [Make the sign of the Cosmic Cross while saying] **In the Name of the Wisdom** [with right hand touch forehead] **and of the Love** [touch heart] **and of the Justice** [touch right shoulder] **and of the Infinite Mercy** [touch left shoulder] **of the One Eternal Spirit.** [circle face] **Amen.** [touch under nose]

4. Purify and seal a piece of black silk large enough to wrap your tarot deck in. Sprinkle blessed salt-water on a piece of black silk while intending to purify it, and then pass it through the blessed incense smoke while intending to seal it to your purpose.

5. Wrap your tarot deck in the black silk cloth, and put it away until needed.

Now that you have a tarot deck which has been consecrated to the god(s) of your heart as a divinatory tool, you will need to know how to divine with them. Below is one of the simpler methods. The only additional skill this process requires of you is the ability to ask good yes/no questions.

Exercise 15: A Simple Tarot Divination Method

1. First determine if the person who requests a divination truly requires and is ready for one.

• Does your client's question necessitate the input of Divinity at this time?

- Are you quite sure that you have exhausted your combined human capabilities to find a satisfactory answer?

- Is the client capable of hearing and abiding by an answer that goes against human desires? (The gods answer all questions, but sometimes the answer is "no!")

2. Take whatever time you need to center, ground, and say a silent prayer to the god(s) of your heart. The prayer should invoke Divinity's aid and protection in the upcoming divination. Your own words to this effect will be far preferable to any formula you could memorize and use.

3. Ask your client to state the question in such a way that it can be answered either with a "Yes" or a "No" and the "Yes" answer represents the preferred answer. (If possible ask the client to also offer up a silent prayer for aid and protection to the god(s) of his or her heart.)

4. Shuffle the tarot deck until you feel the urge to stop.

5. Ask your client to cut the deck one time.

6. Now start at the left hand side of your table and begin laying cards down one on top of the other until you see an ace or reach thirteen cards in that pile.

7. Once you reach an ace or the thirteenth card, start a new pile and again deal out cards one on top of the other until you see an ace or reach thirteen cards in this second pile.

8. Start a new pile and follow the same directions.

9. Now count up the number of aces that show on top of the three piles.

3 Aces = YES

2 Aces = Yes, but (The "but" is represented by the card on top of the remaining pile.)

1 Ace = No, but (The "but" is represented by the cards on top of the remaining piles.)

0 Aces = NO

10. A definite YES or NO must be taken as is and accepted. The "Yes, but" and "No, but" answers indicate ways of turning the situation around or insuring your client's preferred response.

This method of divination is indeed simplistic by nature. As such, it requires tremendous faith on your part and great trust on the part of your client. But then, any time you seek to find out the will of the Divine for yourself or another in a particular situation, both faith and trust will be part of the process.

Step 1 of Exercise 15 is very important. Step 1, Part C, however, may be the most important and most often overlooked aspect of this qualification process. When you seek to know the will of the Divine for yourself or others, you must be willing to take responsibility for the knowledge you seek and find. Although it is perfectly true that we, as human beings, have a great deal of latitude to make choices due to our free will, we cannot ignore with impunity a known Divine directive which we ourselves have sought out.

Let me give you an example of what can happen. One of my clients, Ms. X, spent a good year of her life trying to get up the courage to talk to and hopefully date a certain Mr. Y. She was from a very strict, traditional, and pseudo-aristocratic family while he was from a modern working class family. They met at a gym they both belonged to, and had shared the usual small talk. Every psychic reading I did over the course of that year indicated that "Yes," Ms. X could eventually go out with Mr. Y, but all the work leading up to that event would be on her shoulders. Mr. Y did not seem to be interested in dating anyone right away due to a recently broken engagement. Each reading also indicated that Ms. X could do better by looking for someone else to date (and eventually marry). But she believed she simply had to at least date Mr. Y.

After a year of this frustrating situation, my client found out that Mr. Y was talking to his ex-fiancée. The readings remained the same, but Ms. X (who is quite religious) decided she needed to know if God wanted her to keep working on Mr. Y as she felt driven to do. I explained the difference between a psychic reading and divination to Ms. X and questioned her about how she would react to a definite "no." She swore she could accept that answer. She even said that it would then set her free to look elsewhere for a potential mate. The result of the divination was "no," and she had a very difficult time with it. She knew that I could not encourage her to do something counter to the will of the Divine, yet she could not get rid of her obsession with Mr. Y over night. You can imagine how difficult the next few weeks were for her and for me.

When you do a divination for someone, you must be prepared to see them through any difficulties that result from the knowledge they sought out and got through your work. Up until the time of the divination, so long as the possibility remained open to get a date with Mr. Y, I had been able to encourage Ms. X to try new strategies to make the jump from acquaintance, to friendly acquaintance, to friend, and perhaps even to romantic partner. But the knowledge obtained through the divinatory process tied my hands. All I could then do was help her get over her obsession with Mr. Y, and she really didn't want to do that for quite a long time. Think long and hard before you agree to provide this service for anyone!

CHAPTER 6

COMMUNICATING
WITH THE DEAD

J UST AS YOU DON'T NEED to have particularly well developed psychic abilities to communicate with Divinity, it is not strictly speaking necessary to be a well-trained psychic to communicate with the dead. However, both of these tasks are easier if your psychic abilities are functional.

Over the ages people developed many ways to get in touch with their ancestors. Whole religious systems have been developed around this very human activity. Most of these methods really have two purposes behind them. The first is to seek and find good evidence of the continuing existence of the essence of human beings after physical death. The second is to actually exchange information with loved ones who no longer wear a physical body.

Most people have a very firm hope in some kind of after-life. It matters not whether this hope is the result of a belief in the immortality of the soul in a "one physical life-time is all you get" manner, or a belief in reincarnation and the evolution of the soul godward through many lifetimes' worth of experience and growth. What does matter is how we respond to this hope.

Some of the ways people today choose to communicate with the dead are the following:

1. Seances (the use of trance mediums)

2. Use of a Ouija board

3. Religious services

4. The "George Burns" method: Visiting the gravesite of a deceased loved one and talking to them in just the same way you did when he or she was alive

5. Folk/religious customs such as Day of the Dead observances

Methods 1, 2, and 5 assume that two-way communication between the dead and the living takes place in a literal sense. Methods 3 and 4 leave most of the work up to the person who is living and tend to promote a feeling that the deceased is listening and/or watching. Some modern orthodox religious practices memorializing the dead encourage the living to believe that their loved ones are now at peace and should not be disturbed.

I believe that we do ourselves and our beloved dead a great disservice if we allow our relationship with them to end with their physical death. If we believe, hope, or even feel sure that the essence of who we are survives the process of dying, how can we justify acting as if these people are no longer real to us just because we do not experience them with our physical senses?

Most human beings past a certain age will normally experience two types of events that begin the process of building their hope in the existence of an afterlife. Have you ever seen the corpse that once housed someone you knew well when they were alive or even the remains of a cherished pet? If your experience with either of these common-place events was like that of most people, you recognized rather rapidly that the body in front of you was not the person or pet that you knew and perhaps loved. The body may not even look like the being that you knew (it may seem too small, too one-dimensional). So where did that part you knew go? Have you ever seen the birth of a human or an animal? This often shows the reverse of what you noticed in observing a dead body. You have to look at just the right moment. If you do, you will see what appears to be an inanimate lump of flesh take its first breath and turn into something quite alive. I vividly remember the birth of my first daughter and I will never forget watching a bluish "smoke" gather around her body and join with it just before she let loose with a very deep-voiced yell. In that moment, she changed from a slimy, purplish 9 pound 11 ounce child-shaped bit of flesh to a pink, "life-filled" and very robust baby. My husband didn't see the smoke, but he certainly witnessed the rest with considerable awe (and exhaustion).

Taking all of the above into consideration, it would seem that we should be able to contact and communicate with both those who have passed out of this life through the gate of death and those who are in the process of entering it through the gate of birth. Since we are accustomed to communicating through our physical senses, methods of contact involving seances, Ouija boards, and the like have been developed to allow discarnate entities to communicate in a manner that we can easily understand. These ways of contacting the dead and other spirits brings them into our world by using a living person's vocal cords, hands, or even whole body. Both seances and the use of Ouija boards require some level of voluntary possession on the part of some living person or persons. This necessitates that the people involved take a certain degree of obvious risk. In contrast, direct contact with discarnate entities through such practices as the Dumb Supper (described in Exercise 17, page 73) will not at first provide as concrete communication as any form of voluntary possession, but the presence of a deceased loved one can normally be experienced even by a novice without incurring the level of personal risk that goes along with any level of possession.

There are several different ways to hold a seance. All of them require the presence of someone who is willing and able to allow discarnate spirits to borrow his or her body.

Normally, this person is a trance medium who is able to go into an altered state of awareness known as a deep trance in order to withdraw his or her spirit far enough away from the body so that another spirit may enter and operate it. The obvious risk is that the discarnate spirit may be reluctant to leave after the purpose of the seance has been completed. Spiritualist groups normally guard against this by acquiring the assistance of spirit guides and controls who are asked to screen who or what is allowed access to the seance. These spirit guides and controls are also discarnate entities who may or may not have ever been human at some time during their existences. Working with these beings still leaves your security measures in "hands" other than your own. The not-so-obvious risks involved in this form of spirit communication include the following:

1. The appearance of discarnate entities who are not the beings they purport to be;

2. The trance medium being, in fact, a con artist;

3. Participants in the seance making the mistake of believing that just because the dead no longer wear bodies, they are suddenly all-knowing, all-wise, or completely honest.

Ouija boards are used to encourage communication with discarnate spirits. Normally the board is about the size of a checker board. On it can be found the numbers 0–9, the letters of the alphabet, the words: *Hello*, *Goodbye*, *Yes*, and *No*. It is supposed to be operated by one or more people who are interested in establishing contact with a particular discarnate spirit. The people who operate the board normally quiet themselves in some manner, place their fingers on the planchette (a pointer that easily moves around on the board indicating, words, numbers, or letters to spell out messages), and then ask that particular spirit to communicate using their hands to move the planchette and spell out a message. Most of the time this results in the planchette moving in answer to questions that are put to the spirit who has been contacted.

Ouija boards are subject to all of the same obvious and not-so-obvious risks that we discussed in relation to seances. They also have some other problems associated with them. Ouija boards are most often made by toy companies and sold as either novelties or toys. Needless to say they can be bought and used by people who are simply not prepared to work with them correctly. On top of that, people who don't understand the basics of safe Ouija board use are likely to invite a spirit to visit, fail to adequately screen whatever shows up, and then forget that it is necessary to tell that same spirit to leave when the session is over. (College students are the prime offenders.) This sometimes has some rather unpleasant results such as poltergeist-like activity or nightmares. I can't even begin to count up the number of these messes that I've been called on to help clean up over the years!

If, after reading about the down side of seances and the use of Ouija boards, you still wish to give either of these a go, here is a safe way of doing it.

Exercise 16: Using a Ouija Board Instead of a Trance Medium in a Protected, Séance-Like Setting

1. All who plan to participate should take a purification bath.

• Rid yourself of ordinary dirt with a basic shower.

• Fill your bathtub half full with hot water (as hot as you can stand it). Add one-quarter cup of baking soda and stir.

• Say a prayer of blessing in your own words over the tub. This should indicate your desire to clean and protect yourself spiritually. If you have a hard time thinking of something to say, you might look to the *23rd Psalm* for inspiration.

• Get in and immerse yourself nine times from head to toe. (You may pour water over your head if ducking under is too difficult.)

• Relax in bath until water cools.

• Get out and allow yourself to "air dry." Do not towel off.

2. Prepare an area which at least for a time will be consecrated as a sacred place in which humans (living and dead) and god(s) may meet and communicate in protected peace. This area should have the necessary table, chairs, candles or lights, Ouija board, etc. in place within it.

• Clean this area of all ordinary dirt.

• Use blessed salt-water to cleanse the area of anything that is unnecessary, unwanted, or just plain opposed to the purpose to which the space is being put.

Salt: [Hold dish with salt in it in your left hand and extend the palm of your right hand over it while saying] **As this salt can preserve things in the material world from corruption, so let it be the physical symbol of that which can preserve us from evil and corruption in the spiritual world.** [Make the sign of the Cosmic Cross while saying] **In the Name of the Wisdom** [with right hand touch forehead] **and of the Love** [touch heart] **and of the Justice** [touch right shoulder] **and of the Infinite Mercy** [touch left shoulder] **of the One Eternal Spirit.** [circle face] **Amen.** [with fingers of right hand touch under nose]

Salt in Water: [Sprinkle salt in small vessel of water with right hand, then hold vessel in left hand while extending your right palm over the water while saying] **As this blessed salt dissolves in water, may the two become an intentional agent for cleansing our bodies, minds, and souls as well as this space of all corruption and evil.** [Make the sign of the Cosmic Cross] **In the Name of the Wisdom** [touch forehead] **and of the Love** [touch heart] **and of the Justice** [touch right shoulder] **and of the Infinite Mercy** [touch left shoulder] **of the One Eternal Spirit.** [circle face] **Amen.** [touch under nose]

Purify yourself and the area intended to become a sacred space: [Dip the fingers of your right hand into the blessed salt-water and sprinkle it on yourself. Then take it to the east of your space and walk in a clockwise circle around the space sprinkling it and everything in it with the blessed salt-water.]

• Use blessed incense to seal the area to its intended purpose.

Light incense (of sandalwood or frankincense and myrrh. Use stick incense or charcoal with powdered incense or oil of one of these on top of it. Hold the stick or burner in your left hand while extending your right palm over the smoke while saying: **May these elements of fire and air be blessed with the ability to seal ourselves and this space with the powers of Divine protection, discernment of spirits, and peace.** [Make the sign of the Cosmic Cross while saying] **In the Name of the Wisdom** [with right hand touch forehead] **and of the Love** [touch heart] **and of the Justice** [touch right shoulder] **and of the Infinite Mercy** [touch left shoulder] **of the One Eternal Spirit.** [circle face] **Amen.** [touch under nose]

• Cense yourself and the place while dedicating all to the intended purpose: Go to the east and walk clockwise around the intended sacred space censing everything within it while consciously sealing it to your intended purpose.

3. Have everyone who plans to participate sit down around the table. One person should be prepared to take notes; at least one person should be ready to operate the Ouija board; and one person should be prepared to take the role of leader.

4. Have all join hands and then have the leader talk everyone through the process of centering and grounding.

5. Invoke the god(s) of your heart to guide and guard you all while the Ouija board is being used. Specifically ask that this deity also screen those entities who choose to respond to your invitation to communicate in such a way as to keep those that are fraudulent, violent or harmful in any way, or simply not right in some way, out of your prepared space. Note: You must have great faith in Divinity for this to work well. So, when in doubt—*don't use the Ouija board or perform a seance of any kind*!

6. Go ahead and follow the directions that came with your Ouija board. Be specific about whom you are inviting. Have test questions available to make sure you are speaking to the right spirit. Ask whatever you need to ask.

7. When you are done, *thank* the spirit(s) you have been communicating with and tell them it is now time for them to go back to their rightful abodes. Ask them to do so in such a way that no harm comes to any living being and finish by saying the words "Good-bye, may there be peace between us all forever."

8. Thank Divinity for Its assistance during your work with the Ouija board and spirit communication.

9. Turn on bright lights. Put the room back in its original order. Feed the participants something sweet or something high in protein along with a hot drink of some kind (no alcohol).

10. Discuss what happened and then move on to more mundane matters. Everyone should be in good shape to go back home in about half an hour.

Summoning the dead can be one of the most dangerous operations you undertake as a psychic. Unless your motivation is love, it can tax your physical and psychic resources so much as to be completely debilitating. The Dumb Supper is a folk religious ritual designed to promote communication between you and a deceased loved one. It is set up somewhat like a family dinner and should only be performed in order to invite a beloved dead person to share some time with you. It must never be used with the intent to compel the unwilling or the hostile.

Exercise 17: The Dumb Supper

1. Time this event to coincide with an event that was special to the deceased (birthday, death anniversary, holiday, etc.)

2. At least thirteen days prior to performing this ritual, set up a memorial shrine to the deceased in the west end of the room you plan to use. Use a framed picture of the deceased if you have one. Veil this with a dark cloth. Place flowers and white candles at its sides. Add any objects that once belonged to your dead loved one. All this can be arranged on a small side table.

3. On each of thirteen nights leading up to the Dumb Supper, go to the shrine any time between moonrise and midnight (try to make it the same time each night). Light the candles, unveil the picture, burn some incense of the type described in step 7 below, and sit down facing the portrait. Silently call to the person you wish to contact. Remember all of the good times you shared. Send a message of love and ask the person to visit at a specific date and time in this very place. Then veil the photograph, extinguish the candles, and leave.

4. During the thirteen preparatory days, it is a good idea to isolate yourself as much as possible from the influence of other people. Reserve your affection and attention for the deceased loved one you hope will join you during the Dumb Supper.

On the night of the dumb supper:

5. Fast until the ritual, and take a purification bath as described in Step 1 of Exercise 16.

6. Purify the room and everything to be used with blessed salt-water. (See step 2 Exercise 16.)

7. Seal the room and everything to be used to your intended purpose with blessed incense (one part Dittany of Crete finely chopped, one part Sandalwood oil, and one part crushed rose petals) and follow the ritual for censing in Step 2 of Exercise 16.

8. Just before midnight, arrange the room and do the following:

- Cover a table with a white cloth.

- Place a chair on the east side of the table, facing west, and one on the west side of the table, facing east.

- Place a vase of sweet smelling flowers on the table.

- Light the candles on either side of the picture.

- Start the special incense burning in front of the picture.

- Invoke the god(s) of your heart for aid during this ritual and walk around the room backwards from east to south to west to north. (In this way you begin to walk the pathways of the dead.)

- Set the table. Place the deceased's place setting in the west and yours in the east.

- Bring the food in walking backwards and serve it. (The food and drink should be those favored by the deceased. Serve yourself a normal portion and the deceased a nominal one.)

- At midnight, walk backwards to the picture and unveil it while saying: **"By all that is Holy, I call upon thee by the ties of love, Spirit of** [name of deceased] **to break thy eternal fast with me. So mote it be!"**

- Replenish the incense.

- Walk backwards in a clockwise direction back to your seat and sit down without looking directly at the seat in front of you.

- Eat your dinner in silence. Then walk backwards to the shrine and replenish the incense again.

- Extinguish the candles and walk backwards back to your seat still avoiding looking at the seat in front of you.

- Close your eyes and mentally call the deceased's name three times.

- Keep your eyes shut and mentally welcome your loved one.

• Slowly open your eyes and see what you can see. This will depend a great deal on the level of your psychic development. Even if you see nothing, do not give up. A spirit can manifest in a variety of ways.

• Communicate with your loved one mentally for as long as you like. Enjoy the wordless communion of spirit-to-spirit contact.

• When the experience begins to take on a dream-like quality, it is time to end. Say the following to your loved one: **"It is now time for us to go our separate ways. Please go to your proper place and may there be love between us forevermore. In the Name of the Wisdom and of the Love and of the Justice, and of the Infinite Mercy of the One Eternal Spirit, Amen."**

• Cast a bit more incense on the glowing charcoal as you silently say your good-byes.

The methods of spirit communication which we have covered so far are designed to bring the spirits of the dead to us in one way or another. Most orthodox religious services which honor the dead take our prayers to Divinity on their behalf or our thoughts and memories of the times we shared to them by way of prayer and meditation. My favorite method of communicating with dead loved ones is what I call the "George Burns Method." I gave it this name after listening to him describe his weekly visits to his wife's grave. He used this place much like some of us use telephones. It was the instrument he used to carry his thoughts to his wife. He regularly caught her up on family news and gossip as well as anything else he thought she might want to know about. He said he knew she heard and he could always feel her near him at these times. This method of spirit communication is so normal and loving that very little if anything is likely to go wrong with it. Since it is initiated by the living, the dead can choose to respond or not as they like. There is no pressure on any of the parties in this type of communication and all have the freedom to act as they please.

To my mind the George Burns method is the way to go if your purpose is to simply keep family ties strong. Methods such as the Dumb Supper, or even the seance-like use of the Ouija board, might be better in cases where estrangement has occurred due to staying out of touch for too long or when information is desperately needed that only the dead can give you. In the end, of course, it is entirely up to you as to what methods, if any, you choose to use. Think about it carefully before making your final decision.

CHAPTER 7

RESPONSIBLE USE OF PSYCHIC ABILITIES

HAVE YOU EVER WONDERED why some people respond with fear when they find out someone else is a "psychic?" Perhaps you have written this off by telling yourself that people fear what they don't understand. That is true enough, but where there is smoke there usually is also fire. Psychic abilities can be abused.

Deliberate manipulation of other people's mental, physical, emotional, and/or spiritual environment for purely selfish reasons can be accomplished with relative ease by most psychics should they choose to apply their abilities in this way. Please try the exercise below to find out how easy it can be. I first published this exercise in my book, *The Psychic Self-Defense Personal Training Manual* (published by Samuel Weiser, 1997).

Exercise 18: What is Done to Your Invisible Body Affects Your Visible/Physical Body

1. Have your partner stand comfortably while facing you.

2. Next, have him raise his right arm to shoulder level. He should keep it out straight directly in front of his body while forming his hand into a vertical fist (palm faces to the left, index finger is at the top of the fist).

3. Now position yourself so that your right shoulder is directly in front of the center line of your partner's body (about 2–3 feet in front of him). Stand with your feet shoulder's width apart from each other and bend your knees slightly.

4. Place your right palm on top of your partner's outstretched right fist and ask him to resist upwards as you press downwards. This will establish the initial strength relationship between the two of you. If your partner is considerably weaker than you are, you may use 1 or 2 fingers to press down with instead of your entire palm (see figure 3, page 79).

5. Next take your right hand and cup it with your palm facing away from your partner. Bring this hand down the center line of your partner's body (about 4 inches from his body surface) from head to groin level. At this point your right hand scoops away from your partner and past the left side of your body before arching up and then back over your head to the original position in front of your partner's head (see figure 4, page 80). Repeat this with increasing speed 3-6 more times while visualizing yourself as stretching your partner's normally invisible psychic body/aura out and away from him. Finally, throw your right arm directly away from your partner's body while visualizing yourself hanging the outer edge of his psychic body up on the opposite wall or some other appropriate place several feet or more away from the two of you.

6. Now repeat step 4 and notice the difference. Your partner's arm should not be able to resist your pressure as well as it did originally and may indeed simply drop to his side (see figure 5, page 81). Why might this happen?

7. Stand facing your partner (front to front) and place your two thumbs together upon the center of his forehead (third

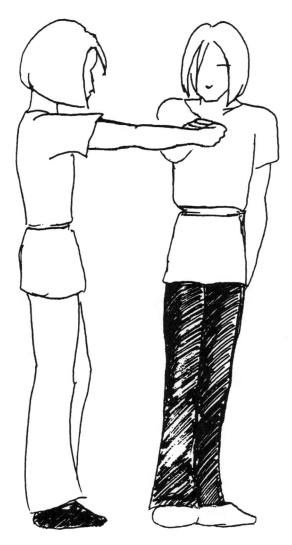

Figure 3. Strength testing.

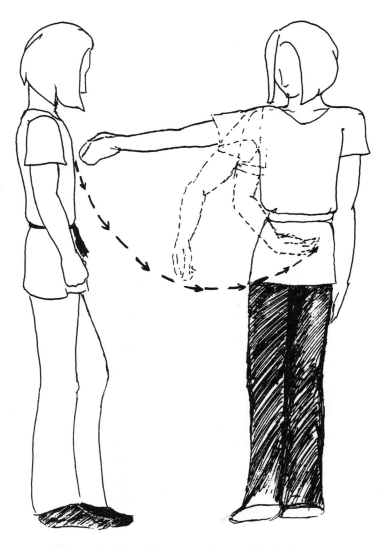

Figure 4. Stretching out the psychic body.

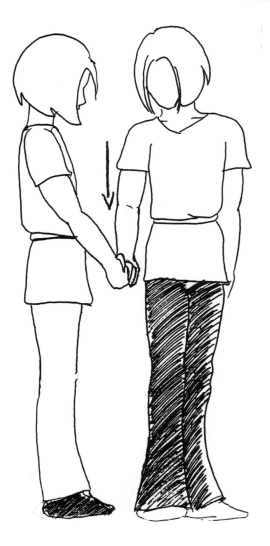

Figure 5. A second strength test shows that the subject's arm can be moved more easily when the psychic body is weakened.

eye area) while wrapping your fingers lightly around his head. Mentally unhook your partner's psychic body from wherever you left it and allow it to flow back through your body and thumbs into its original position (extending 6–8 inches from your partner's physical body). Don't worry if it happens to settle slightly closer to your partner's body than it did originally (see figure 6, page 83).

8. Repeat step 4 and notice the difference. Your strength relative to your partner's should be back to it original relationship, or your partner may feel slightly stronger than he did initially. Ask yourself why this happens.

9. Repeat step 5 while asking your partner to mentally assert the following: "This is my energy and you may not take it away from me!"

10. Repeat step 4 and notice the result. Your strength relative to that of your partner's should have remained in its original relationship.

11. Allow your partner to try all of the above on you.

12. Try the same exercise using only visualizations and not the circular hand motions as you stretch your partner's psychic body.

Most people who develop their psychic potential are decent human beings with average to above average intelligence and moral values. However, greater power always brings with it greater challenges and greater temptations.

As your psychic abilities mature, it is important that you remain aware of your personal motivations. For instance, are you using your ability to read cards merely to draw attention to yourself in social gatherings? Do you ask people when they were born in order to understand them better or because you can gain some advantage over them

Figure 6. Returning the subject's psychic body to its original position.

by using your knowledge of Numerology? If you have decided to become a professional psychic, how much service are you providing for the money you are charging?

Romance and sexual encounters are very susceptible to conscious or unconscious psychic manipulation. It is not at all difficult to "enchant" someone with simply the hint that you have developed your psychic potential to an unusual degree. Knowing a person's full name and birthdate or doing a tarot card reading can provide you with innumerable insights on which you could capitalize if you chose to do so.

For all of these reasons it is very important to maintain strict ethical standards when it comes to your interaction with clients in particular and all people in general. You may feel that the rules that I suggest are overly idealistic, but humans and especially humans who have trained their psychic abilities need ideals to live up to if they are to evolve godward rather than devolve toward exploitative materialism.

If you agree with the point of view that Divinity acts upon us through those who enter our spheres of influence, then it is not unreasonable to ask you to honor the Divine in all those whom you meet. You do not honor anyone or anything by exploiting them. Casual sexual contact merely gratifies the ego and the physical body. Casual sexual contact exploits another human being and dishonors the Divine spark in both participants by virtually ignoring It. You may, of course, want to challenge that statement because you think that I have not adequately defined "casual sexual contact." But the definition is quite simple. If you are exploiting another human being through sexual contact which requires no real relationship with that person, then you are engaging in casual sex. Therefore I recommend that you avoid that behavior as one way to avoid abusing your psychic gifts.

Psychic abilities are gifts from Divinity to humankind, but they are no guarantee of either moral behavior, holiness, or religious genius. It is perfectly possible to be psychically powerful while being weak in other ways. For exactly this reason we have noted that it is wise to offer your psychic abilities to the god(s) of your heart on a daily basis.

When you allow the will of the Divine in you to direct the use of your psychic powers, you will always do what is right. To ensure that you are indeed doing this, you need to make sure your psyche is fit and rested. Deity can't use a channel which isn't kept clear for the passage of Its energy. Here are three practices which should form a basic spiritual fitness program: commune with the god(s) of your heart daily; examine your conscience at least twice a week and make amends when necessary; pray constantly.

Another way to help yourself stay on track ethically is to ritually dedicate yourself and your abilities to Divinity through a ceremonial practice known as initiation. The Cup or Chalice is a Western symbol of wisdom, understanding, compassion, and psychic abilities melded with spiritual strength. The Cup can be used for the practice of *scrying*. As with most methods of focusing psychic abilities, scrying can be used solely for the purpose of mundane psychic readings or for the practice of Divination. Below you will find the script for a beautiful Initiation for those who would use the Cup wisely.

This ritual was written by Wm. G. Gray for the Sangreal Sodality and entrusted to my care. In my opinion it will serve humanity best by being available to the public at large. You are welcome to use it "as is" or re-work it to suit your religious tradition.

Initiation of the Cup

Participants in this Ritual:

> Questioner
> Candidate
> Initiating Officer
> Preceptor (Master of Ceremonies)
> Pontifex

The Ritual

[The Candidate knocks four times at the outside door to the Temple.]

Questioner: **Who knocks?**

Candidate: **One who seeks communion with themselves, this Company, and the Eternal Gods.**

Questioner: **In what condition are you?**

Candidate: **I thirst.**

Questioner: **For water or for wine?**

Candidate: **I would drink the Wine of Wisdom and the Water of Eternal Life.**

Questioner: **Know you their price?**

Candidate: **Myself. I am prepared to pay.**

Questioner: **What have you to contain this dear and deathless draught?**

Candidate: **Nothing.**

Initiating Officer: **Nothing is the largest Cup existing since it holds all things within itself. We will exchange this for you with a lesser yet a kinder Cup in common use among us in the Mysteries. Enter, bearing nothing with you, and we will accept it.**

[Candidate enters, takes position before West point.]

Initiating Officer: **We greet you gladly, yet we see you plainly have a Cup already in yourself most evident within your mortal body. We cannot proceed beyond this point until you tell us what this is.**

Candidate: **My heart.**

Preceptor: Even so, your human heart holds all that is most precious in yourself and they who love you—life itself. An empty heart is dead. The heart has ever been the sign of love through every level. As your heart is bound by blood to every portion of your body through the Links of Life, so is Love the Blood of Being, linking through its Blessed Bond the Highest God with all that Being is. Remember this before all else.

> In the Body, Blood
> In the Soul, Love
> In the Spirit, Life

All are held as one within the Chalice of Creation. Therefore we say to you: become a Living Cup yourself and hold Divine and human Love together. Thus will you be a blessed Chalice from whence God and man partake of one another. This is the Inside of your Cup. What is the outer sign?

Candidate: My hollowed hands.

Preceptor: Our oldest drinking vessel, and the symbol of donation or reception as the hands are full or empty. Life is a matter of both giving and receiving and the purpose of a Cup is to fulfill these functions. In your hands, you hold as much or little as yourself, and you in turn are held within the Hands of God among the rest of us. Being within Being beyond our understanding. Remember, when you hold within your human hands the blessed Chalice of the Holy Mysteries, that it is but an outer symbol made from metal by the hands of men. The true and living Cup around it is no less than your own hands and you that use them for this sacred purpose, even a Greater Cup is formed around yourself by the Eternal Hands of God who uses you with a Divine Intention. This is your Outer Cup and its significance. Think well upon these things within your Cup of Consciousness and it will never be empty. Which Quarter of the Worlds has harmony associated with the Cup?

Candidate: The Western Quarter with its Element of Water, Angel of the Horn and all that appertains thereto.

Preceptor: Therefore let us ask the special blessing of the Holy Ones appointed to the West upon this present enterprise.

All: So mote it be. Amen.

Pontifex: Thou Great Invisibles whom we approach with reverence through the Western Gateway of the Inner World, connect thy consciousness with ours in the Communion of the Cup, and let us meet each other in the Way of Wisdom through the medium of Love. Here on Earth, our hands and hearts are opened before Heaven. Fill them with fervent and unfailing faith in the Divine Compassion which encompasses our beings. Another Cup of the Most Holy Mysteries is forming now among us on this Earth who are Companions of the Living Light. Prosper thou this blessed work, O Holy Ones who dwell forever in the boundless Ocean of Eternal Love. Pour forth upon us all the Grace of God Most Merciful and Mighty, so that there may be set forever in the heart and hands of this, thy supplient, the Sacred Symbol of the Cup, and open thou the way that lies before us through the blessed Waters of Immortal Life.

All: So mote it be. Amen.

Preceptor: Be blessing bidden on the water that sets forth the Symbol of the Infinite Eternal Ocean of our Origin whence we emerged in Primal Purity.

Pontifex: Let there be a Firmament in the midst of the waters, dividing the waters from the waters, for that which is above is like to that which is below, and that which is below is like to that which is above. O thou Supreme One of the Sea, who hast the keys to the floodgates of heaven and dost confine the waters of the underworld in the caverns of Earth. Ruler of the deluge and floods of the springtime who dost unseal the sources of rivers and fountains, and dost ordain moisture which is like the blood of Earth to become the sap of plants, Thee we adore and Thee we invoke. Speak unto us, thine inconstant and unstable creatures in the great tumults of the sea and we shall tremble before Thee. Speak unto us also in the murmur of limpid waters, and we shall yearn for thy love. O Immensity into which flow all the rivers of life to be continually reborn in Thee. O Ocean of Infinite Perfection. Height which reflects Thee in the depth, and depth which exalts Thee to the heights, lead us into true life by thine intelligence and love. Lead us into immortality by sacrifice, that we may be worthy one day to offer Thee water, blood, and tears, for the remission of our sins.

Amen.

Preceptor: Here is the water. Where is the Cup you need to bear it with you?

Candidate: I do not know.

Preceptor: Then seek, and you will find. Ask, and you will receive. Knock and it will open unto you. Now set forth upon your quest for the Most Holy Grail as every other mortal must. Pursue the Path of Light and pausing at each Quarter cry; "I seek the Grail. Who holds it here?" Await the answer, obey instructions, and abide the issue. God be with you. Go.

[Candidate proceeds to the North and calls.]

North: **The stern and strong relentless ones have failed to take the Grail by force. We hold it not. Pass by upon the Right Hand Path.**

[Candidate goes to the East and calls.]

East: **The keen, intelligent, and clever ones have failed to win the Grail by wit. We hold it not. Pass by upon the Right Hand Path.**

[Candidate goes to the South and calls.]

South: **The subtle and seductive ones have failed to steal the Grail by guile. We hold it not. Pass by upon the Right Hand Path.**

[Candidate goes to the West and calls.]

West: **The Wise ones of the West are linked to one another in the Grail by Love alone. We are held in it, and hold it not from any soul that finds it for themselves where it lies hidden in the unknown depths of their own being. Stay and search.**

[A reflective pool is indicated in which the Candidate can see his or her face.]

Preceptor: **See how Light reflected from the surface of a peaceful pool reveals the face of an onlooker to themselves as in a mirror. Nothing more. Never be satisfied with mere appearances. Plunge through the outer image of yourself and find the Inner Truth that lies beneath it, safely at the bottom of the Well of Wisdom.**

[Candidate plunges arm, finds Cup. As it is brought to light, all respond.]

All: **Glory to the Grail that comes from darkness into light!**

[While Candidate dries the Cup on the towel provided, the following homily is read.]

Preceptor: **Remember always that you found this Cup upon the very point where you began your pointless quest in search of it. Had you looked with Inner Spiritual Sight, instead of being deceived by outward images, you would have seen it where it lay within your reach. All you learned upon your pilgrimage was where you need not look for what you sought. From this lesson, learn to look for Truth at first within yourself, before you waste your life in seeking elsewhere for a truth you hold within yourself already. Blessed indeed are those becoming Bearers of the Cup. Be it proclaimed of potency and purpose.**

Pontifex: **Behold! I am the Cup of Cosmos, and entire Creation lies within my compass. All things exist in Me not I in them. Force flows into my Form. I hold and hallow every life as one within the Chalice of my Consciousness, for Omniscience is mine. Existence and experience of every kind is in me, for I am the draught of Death or Immortality. On Earth I hold the Oceans or the raindrops. In man I am Capacity of every kind. In Heaven I present the Path of Love. In God, I am the hollowed Hand of the Compassionate made manifest in Mercy. Trust me.**

All: **So mote it be. Amen.**

Preceptor: **Behold the Symbol of the Cup that shows Divine and human Love participating in Eternal Life together. Would you possess this? None can possess the**

Cup. We must Become it. That is the only way of owner-ship. For the love we bear you in the Holy Mysteries, we gladly offer you this earthly emblem if you will agree to take the oath that we must now administer in modern terms according to most ancient custom. Hear its terms.

I, _____, accept this Chalice of the Mysteries according to my Light of Understanding and the Love to God and Humankind I bear within me. The honor of this Cup shall be mine own, and as I deal with it, so may the Hands of Heaven deal with me. I will not permit this ves-sel to be used impurely or profanely, under penalty of being excluded from companionship and love by God and man alike until I earn full pardon for such spiritual shame. In this Cup I will commune with the Eternal Spirit of the Living God as I shall be instructed in the Holy Mysteries. With it I will continue and commemorate the Links of Love I hold with my Companions of the Blessed Bond both in this human world or out of it. Through this Cup I seek the All-Compassionate Who ut-tered me at my beginning. Be it unto me according to that Word. May the Holy Hosts of Heaven help me keep this word of mine I pledge to the Omniscient One before this Company both visible and hidden witnesses of what I promise through the Sacred Symbol of the Cup.

Standing thus before the Cup between the Pillars of acceptance or refusal, you must freely choose your way. This is the Law: In Perfect Love, do what thou wilt. No penalty attaches to you for refusal at this point except the natural result from loss of contact with the meaning of this moment. How say you to this Cup and what it holds for you from this time forth. Yes or No?

[If Candidate answers "Yes," then:]

Preceptor: Take this Cup within your hands, and with it take the Oath as we repeat it. Remember that it lies be-tween yourself and God alone. We are but witnesses.

Now say with us, for we too are remembering our Oaths with you.

[After the Oath, Companions give the Hailing Signs.]

All: **Hail to, and Blessed be the birth of one more Cup within the Holy Mysteries of Eternal Life and Everlasting Love. All hail.**

Preceptor: **Now let us learn the usage of the Cup, that purpose may be turned to practice. What must first be learned of any Art?**

Candidate: **Its Elements.**

Preceptor: **This Art is no exception to that rule. Therefore, let us approach each element in turn around the Path of Light in search of Wisdom. On Earth we are, with Earth let us commence the circle.**

[At North, the Cup is filled with black and white particles and consecrated.]

Pontifex: **We call upon Thee by thy best beloved and oldest Name, O Mother Earth, without whose boundless generosity the race of man would surely perish from thy face. Enter into this, thine element, and seal it with thine own stability. Manifest thy meaning by the very motion of the world beneath our feet, and may thy Gracious Ones come forth with glory. Be thou consecrated, faithful creature of the Earth, through the power and in the service of the Single Self-Existence whose inherent particles we are.**

Preceptor: **Now take the Cup, and empty it with care completely over this design. At the same time, empty out your mind while you propose some problem or select** some special subject. Tap the quarters of the tablet thus, then meditate some moments on the meaning of the mandala you meet within your mental vision. In conclusion, tell us briefly your impressions.

[Candidate obeys.]

Preceptor: Yet why is the Cup not empty? There is something in it that remains invisible. Know you what it is? Shape and Form remain within the Cup. Can you empty that from the interior? Impossible? Then let us take our form-filled Cup unto the East and try once more to clear it.

[Suitable music or chanting may be used between Points.]

[In the East, a small quantity of equal black and white feathers are put in the Cup, a trace of perfume touched inside rim, and Air invoked.]

Pontifex: We call upon Thee O Formative One of our existence Who didst breathe into the soul of man the Breath of Life, and from whose spoken Word above the Ocean of the Infinite, all that lives began. Enter into this, thine Element, and let it vibrate with the earthly echoes of thy Heavenly Voice. Let thy winds of truth awake us with the motion of their inner message, manifesting thine intentions throughout all the worlds. Be thou consecrated, faithful creature of the air, through the power and in the service of the One Eternal Life whose single breaths we are.

Preceptor: Now take the Cup and hold it thus. Concentrate your consciousness upon some single point, inhale, then completely empty body, mind, and soul together with the Cup by one swift outward breath across the rim. As feathers fly and fall, so note and meditate some moments on the outcome and expound most briefly your impressions.

[Candidate obeys. Music if needed.]

Preceptor: **Why is not the Cup completely empty? There are yet invisibles within it. Know you what they are? Perfumed air remains within the Cup. Empty that, and we will go our ways in peace. Impractical? Let us take our cup of form and perfumed air into the South and try once more to clear it.**

[In the South, a red votive lamp is lit and put into the Cup, and incense kindled on the side altar. Later, all lights but the Cup are extinguished.]

Pontifex: **We call upon Thee O Father of all, radiant with thine illuminating rays. O Unseen Parent of the Sun, pour forth thy Light giving power and energize thy Divine Spark. Enter into this flame, and let it be agitated by the breath of thy Holy Spirit, manifest thy Power, and open for us the hidden Temple of the Light this flame conceals. Be thou consecrated, faithful creature formed from Fire, through the Power, and in the service of the Supreme Single Light whose individual scattered sparks we are. Now kneel in peace a while, and contemplate the Light that shines through silent scented smoke. Be minded as you will, but let your sight be of the soul and pass the barrier of mere appearances. Look not at, but through the Light. Be inwardly illuminated. When your vigil is accomplished, rise, and take this taper, lighting from the Cup the altar lights and others. Try thus to empty Light completely from yourself and the Cup.**

[Candidate obeys.]

Preceptor: **Is the Cup not empty yet? What lingers in it now? If vision operates within a Cup, then there is Light inside it. Empty out its light, and let us go our way. This is impossible. You have already kindled infinitely greater** quantities of Light from this one Cup than you could ever empty from it. Let us take our form-filled, air-perfumed, illuminated Cup with us unto the West and try again to clear it.

[In the West, the Cup is filled with water on which some vervain leaves are floated.]

Pontifex: We call upon Thee O Thou Mighty One that dwellest ever in the Waters of Eternal Life. Flow Thou in freedom through us, so that we may be fulfilled in thine Infinity. Enter into this, thine Element and move it with thy Mercy and Compassion. For the Sun is its Father, the Moon its Mother, and the wind hath carried it in the womb thereof. It ascendeth from Earth to Heaven, and again it descendeth from Heaven to Earth. Be Thou consecrated, faithful creature formed from water, by the Power, and in the service of, the One Eternal Ocean of Immortal Life whose separated scattered drops we are.

Preceptor: Take now the Cup, and contemplate its contents, studying the surface patterns carefully for information through your intuition. See inside yourself the Fountain of Eternal Wisdom, and catch but one drop of it within the Cup you bear between your hands.

Take what thoughts may come to you, then empty them completely from you with this Cup at the same instant. Look at the disposition of what leaves may still remain, and make some meaning out of this. Clean the Cup properly, and then return it.

[Candidate obeys.]

Preceptor: Why is the Cup not empty yet? What yet remains invisibly within it? Sound can be clearly heard within the Cup, therefore it cannot be completely empty.

Take it and empty out all sounds from it, and let us then continue. Is this not possible? Then let us keep our form-filled, air-perfumed, illuminated, sounding Cup and pause awhile for thought.

[Candidate may sit for the following lecture.]

Questioner: Have you learned the usage of the Cup?

Candidate: [Anwers either yes, no, or I'm not sure.]

Preceptor: You have learned some of its associations and a mild misuse or so. Nothing more. Never use a fully consecrated Cup for gratifying curiosity or suchlike oracles. Keep what is called a *vulgar* vessel for such practices if you would perform them. Remember that the more you tried to empty out the Cup, the more was realized to be within it? Even so, the more you pour forth from yourself the more will reach you from the Spiritual Source inside you that is inexhaustible. Truly it is said; "Blessed are the empty, for they shall be filled." It is really easier for you to empty every ocean on this Earth with that small Cup, than empty all that lies within yourself beneath your surface. Never forget that.

Questioner: Now that we have covered every Quarter with the Cup, what Points remain?

Candidate: The Height and Depth that are the Pivots of the Poise between Divine and Earthly Life.

Questioner: Let us approach humanity before presuming to contact Divinity. How many senses have you as a bodied being?

Candidate: Five—sight, hearing, touch, taste, smell.

Preceptor: **Therefore, if you would consciously relate yourself with other humans, you must do so with those senses, for they are your standard of reality in mortal life. Look at me. Listen to me. Touch me. Answer, am I real to you? If you saw and heard and touched Divine Ones with such clarity of consciousness, you would swiftly learn that they are far more real than I appear in my mortality. You have inner senses that approximate those of your body. These must be awakened and co-ordinated through the Symbol of the Cup, which signifies the vessel of your Inner Being. Just as your mortal body is your outer vehicle. Use your outer senses to awaken Inner ones. Look literally inside the Cup, and open up your Inner Eye of vision. Listen in actuality with your ear against its edge, and through the outer silence, you will hear the Inward Voice. Hold the Cup between your hands and make its shape within your mind, the form of what you seek, or Who seeks you. Savor wine within the Cup as an experience of ecstasy or Love between your soul and the Divine One whom you give it to thereby. This is the central secret of the Cup which it must teach you of itself. The mouth of man is meaningless herein, nor can it give the Kiss of the Divine One that bestows Immortal Life.**

The Cup is for communion and communication with the holiest and highest conscious Life you can contact by whatsoever name you call upon it.

Make its Symbol mean just that to you for purpose and in practice, then leave the rest to Higher Hands than ours.

All: **So mote it be.**

Questioner: **How do you pledge a Cup-Companion?**

Candidate: **With a well-meant word across a Cup extended to them at the level of the lips.**

Preceptor: Tradition tells that our Originator raised his Holy Head above the Waters of Eternal Life, and when his lips had cleared the surface, spoke the Word of Light that brought us into being. Since the image that He saw reflected by the Water in the Light was his Own Countenance, it has been taught that He created Man in his Own Likeness. In like manner therefore, pledge yourself unto the Holy One within your Cup. As He saw you in the beginning, you should see Him in the end through your reflection in the wine your Cup contains. Even as you were created by the Word above the Water, so create within your consciousness a contact with the Great Divine One by your Word above the Wine.

[Four strokes on gong then short silence.]

Preceptor: Remember also to commemorate Companions of the Blessed Bond within your Cup, whether they are in or out of bodied being. Whosoever cannot find Divinity through fellow humans, surely will not meet the Holy Ones within themselves. The Gateway to the Heavens opens from this Earth. No Celebration of the Cup can be complete without a Circle of Companionship around it, whether they are present in their persons, or summoned by you in the Spirit. Be mindful of the clause within the Blessed Covenant which says: "Where two or three are gathered in My Name, there will I be within the midst of them."

Questioner: How many separate Cups contain experience on Earth?

Candidate: Two. The Cup of Sorrow and the Cup of Joy.

Preceptor: Here are their representatives beside the Pillars. Taste of each, and understand what must be undergone between extremities of pain and pleasure.

[Candidate should be warned to only sip each of the intensely bitter and sweet cups.]

Preceptor: **See! Each is unsatisfactory by itself, and arouses an antipathy that urges you to seek another opposite sensation. So turns relentlessly the Crucifying Wheel of Birth and Death that binds you by attachment to self-seeking incarnations on this Earth. Free yourself from this constraining circle by partaking of the pure Water of Immortal Life that waits for you upon the Middle Way within the Heavenly Chalice of Contentment.** [Offering Water:] **In the name of liberating Love, take, drink, live.**

[Candidate drinks.]

Preceptor: **Even as the Water and the Wine of Earth and Heaven interchange with one another, so let the Cup that brought the Body bear the Blood. So mote it be. Let the Cup be duly consecrated to the Sacred Service.**

[Here the Cup is solemnly borne to the East of the altar by the Pontifex.]

Pontifex: **In the Name of the Wisdom, and of the Love, and of the Justice, and of the Infinite Mercy of the One Eternal Spirit.**

All: **Amen.**

Pontifex: **O Thou Supreme and Perfect One by whose Omnipotent Creative Craft all things are made, hear Thou the Will within these words and set thy seal of truth upon them. Acknowledging our earthly faults and insufficiencies, we do admit our use of artifice and symbols to assist us in approaching Thee as vessels seeking to be filled with thine encompassing and boundless Love. We bring to Thee for blessing and for consecration, this most an-**

cient Symbol of a Cup, by which is signified the Link of Love among us in the Covenant of thy Most Holy Mysteries. Once, sacrificial blood outpoured upon an altar made the Mystic Bond between Divine and human Life. Now upon a Path made pure by progression, we offer up upon our altars an oblation of Wine of Wisdom in the Chalice of Compassion. This becomes for us the Blessed Blood by which we are united in thy Holy Spirit, and belong to Thee and one another as a faithful family of thy begetting. In this Cup, we see the bowl to signify thy Heavenly Spirit above, its base our own mortality on Earth below, and the supporting stem to be our means of meeting Thee in common union. Seal Thou with us this Symbol, and accept it for thy sacred service, set apart from others of its kind for this pure purpose. From this time henceforth may it be counted with the company of every Cup that constitutes thy Grail of Grace on Earth.

[Touching the bowl of the cup] **Blessed be the Holy One of Heaven holding us within his hollowed hands.**

[Touching the base of the cup] **Blessed be Divinity on Earth made manifest through mankind.**

[Touching the stem of the cup] **Blessed be the strong straight path of perfect faith between Divine and human Life.**

All: **Glory to the Grail made greater by more Love Divine among us.**

[Short silence. At each blessing there is a gong stroke. Afterwards, while the lead seal of consecration is being affixed under the base, an anthem or suitable hymn is sung, and incense offered.]

Pontifex: **Be the Covenant completed by the Will within the Word above the Wine. So mote it be. Blessed be the Holy Mystery of Water, Wine, and Blood becoming One in Everlasting Life.**

[Water and wine are put into the chalice by the Pontifex.]

Pontifex: **As I fill the Cup, so be it unto me fulfilled. None truly gain the Grail of Grace save they who fill it by their life-blood offered up with all their hearts within their souls. This is the Wine of Wisdom in the Chalice of Compassion. Fill then the Cup, to be fulfilled therein.**

[Candidate fills cup.]

Candidate: **This is the Wine of Wisdom in the Chalice of Compassion.**

Pontifex: **Not spilling vital blood in senseless sacrifice upon a stone, but bearing it within our veins alive as an oblation to the Living God, we offer up ourselves upon this altar as most willing Victims of the Perfect One whose Presence we approach this moment, praying: O Thou Immortal and Eternal Spirit of the Ever-Loving God in Whom we live unceasingly, take Thou into Thyself this wine we offer as our very blood, that it may verily become in us a vehicle of thy Most Blessed Being. Do with us as thou wilt, that our wills may be truly thine in Heaven and on Earth. Accept Thou us, as Thou wouldst be accepted in this Holy Cup wherein we pledge ourselves to Thee and to each other in thy Presence. Unite us in Thyself O Omnipresent and Omniscient Living Spirit who most truly art both God and man in one another. Even as thy Word above the Water brought us into mortal life, so let our word above the Wine now bring us into thine Immortal Love.**
     O. U. H. A. I. M.*

[Gong, silence.]

---

*The meaning of this becomes clear to each person as it is vibrated and
meditated upon.

[The Companions have gathered kneeling around the Candidate. The Pontifex kneels and passes the Chalice to the nearest Companion. Lightwards, it goes round the Circle till the Pontifex drinks and passes it to the Candidate, who empties and holds the Cup. There may be very quiet meditational music.]

Candidate: **Glory be to Thee, O Spirit of the Living God made manifest among mankind.**

Pontifex: [lays right hand over Cup] **For no less holy purpose may this Cup be ever used again. In the Name of the Wisdom and of the Love and of the Justice and of the Infinite Mercy of the One Eternal Spirit. Amen.**
Blessed is the Cup containing Nothing for it shall be filled by All.

All: **Blessed be the LIGHT beyond all Being.**

[All repeat the next response after each blessing spoken by the Pontifex.]

Forever Blessed be the Living Spirit. Amen.

Pontifex: **Blessed be the Breathing of Origination.**

All: **Forever Blessed be the Living Spirit. Amen.**

Pontifex: **Blessed be Eternal Wisdom.**

Blessed be Omniscient Understanding.

Blessed be Perpetual Compassion.

Blessed be Almighty Justice.

Blessed be Transcendent Beauty.

Blessed be Unceasing Victory.

Blessed be Surpassing Glory.

Blessed be Infallible Foundation.

Blessed be all Life throughout the Kingdom.

Preceptor: May you be granted every grace and gift of God that you are able to accept. As you make a Cup within yourself, it will be filled according to its nature and capacity. Therefore be ever cautious how you open out your heart and soul, for as you hollow them they are refilled. Should you make room for what is wrong, that surely follows. So does goodness if you rightly form your Inner Chalice. Whatever you would have in life, become its Cup or mold, and it will enter you. Be well advised to make yourself into a Cup which may be rightly filled by true Divinity alone. Hold Nothing yours, and you have more than you will ever need. Meditate upon this Mystery, for out of Nothing you came forth, and into Nothing will you surely go. Therefore hold Nothing more precious than All, and if you would contain this Truth in its own terms—Turn down an empty Cup!

[Inverts Chalice in Candidate's hands.]

Preceptor: In the Name of the Wisdom and of the Love and of the Justice and of the Infinite Mercy of the One Eternal Spirit. Amen.

[Gong. Sign of Silence. All still. Close Temple according to custom.]

CHAPTER 8

ADVANCED APPLICATIONS
OF PSYCHIC ABILITIES

S O FAR WITHIN THIS book you have been enlight-
ened in a variety of ways concerning your psychic potential, its development, and use. Below is a brief
reminder of the things you learned as you read this book
and worked with the exercises that were presented.

1. Your psychic potential is as *natural* to your makeup as a
human being as are your five physical senses, intelligence,
and physical strengths and weaknesses (Introduction).

2. You can awaken and exercise your psychic abilities
through the processes of centering, grounding, awakening
awareness within your physical body, and psychically sensing time (exercises 1–4 in chapter 1).

3. One way to focus your psychic ability is through the
tools of tarot and Numerology (chapters 2 and 3).

4. There is a difference between psychic abilities and spiritual power (chapter 4).

5. The tarot may be used for either psychic readings or divination (chapter 5).

6. Always remember the importance of spiritual development (chapters 4 and 7).

7. There are appropriate ways to use your psychic and spiritual abilities to communicate with the dead (chapter 6).

8. Psychic abilities can be both used and abused (chapter 7).

9. You can ensure responsible use of your psychic abilities (chapter 7).

Please take the time to review any of the above subjects that you may have skimmed over on your way to this chapter. They provide the necessary foundation for the more advanced applications of your psychic skills which I will be discussing next. Whether you plan to work as a professional psychic or just wish to hone your skills to help yourself and others, you will need to work on several skills which will help you make wise use of your psychic impressions. Earlier in this book I told you that the ability to interpret information gained through the psychic senses correctly was the key to becoming a good psychic. Intuitive impressions rise out of the subconscious mind by way of the psychic senses. Interpretation depends on the reasoning ability of your conscious or rational mind.

You have already learned the basics of accessing information through the use of your psychic senses and the fundamentals of interpretation. These skills were taught to you in chapters 1–3. Working with patterns of symbols whether they be tarot cards, numbers, dreams, or the like is what allows you to "read" psychic information in a fluent manner. Recognizing areas that require special attention and handling within a client's life is the skill that allows you to communicate your findings in a useful and wise manner. I will demonstrate both of these skills through an analysis of a Numerology chart used in conjunction with a tarot card spread.

Normally, a Birth Name Chart is interesting but not particularly useful after you have entered the second Major Cycle of Life. By this time, your natural abilities have been extended by adding learned abilities; your beginning motivations have been altered by circumstances; and your dreams have changed accordingly. It is also true that if you are firmly out of the first Major Cycle of Life, you have learned the lessons indicated by the numbers that are covered by the birth name and those that are overemphasized. That is why, if you came to me as a first-time client, I would begin by asking for your date of birth. If you were at least in the Transition Stage between the first and second Major Cycles of your life (two years before the end of the first Major Cycle to two years after the beginning of the second Major Cycle) then I would normally work with the Birthdate Chart rather than the Birth Name *and* Birthdate Charts. The reason for this is practical. The Birth Name Chart will refer mostly to the person you used to be rather than the person you have become. There are occasions when I might go back to your Birth Name Chart under these conditions, but they are rare. I use the Birthdate Chart to give me information about what types of circumstances you have dealt with in the past, are dealing with in the present, and may be encountering in the future.

I will then normally work with the tarot cards to see how you will be responding to your future circumstances unless you change something about the way you normally approach opportunities and challenges in life. Please reread that last sentence. This is yet another reminder that what hasn't happened doesn't necessarily *have* to happen, no matter what my psychic senses are suggesting to me. You, as the client, always have an opportunity to change your behavior, attitude, etc. in order to change an unwanted outcome. Anything that hasn't already occurred can be altered or avoided entirely.

One of my clients, Mr. P, had the following Birthdate Chart when I did a reading for him in January, 1986.

Birthdate: April 4, 1930
Destiny = 3

MAJOR CYCLE	PINNACLES	CHALLENGES
1 = 4 (Birth–1963)	1 = 8 (Birth–1963) (1991–1999)	1 = 0 (Birth–Death)
2 = 4 (1964–1986)	2 = 8 (1964–1972)	2 = 0 (1964–Death)
	3 = 7 (1973–1981)	
3 = 4 (1986–Death)	4 = 8 (1982–1990)	3 = 0 (1964–Death)

After taking a couple of minutes to do the arithmetic for his chart, I took the time to center and ground. (This takes only a few seconds once you get the hang of it.) Then I let my psychic senses zero in on the parts of the chart that would be important to interpret. Finally I began analyzing the chart. To practice what you have learned, take the time to center and ground, then gaze at Mr. P's Birthdate Chart and see what you pick up as being important. Remember this reading was done in 1986.

When I did this reading, three aspects stood out to my psychic senses as being very important:

1. 1986 is right in the middle of the Transition Period between the second and third Major Cycles of Life.

2. 1986 is a turning point in a nine-year cycle which started in 1982.

3. Mr. P has a triple "0" Challenge.

So what does all this mean? The following is how I began the reading:

> Mr. P, right now you are in what is known as the Transition Period between your second and third Major Cycles of Life. In Numerology there are

only three Major Cycles. The first one builds the foundation for who you are going to be and what you are going to do by the usual growing-up, learning, and maturation processes. It lasts between twenty-seven and thirty-five years. You had a thirty-three-year first Major Cycle. This means that it took at least that long to get enough breadth and depth of experience to begin to use your abilities to their best advantage in the world. It also means that the last time that there was as much chaos in your life as there is right now would have been between the years 1961 and 1966. That was when you made the transition between the foundation-laying first Major Cycle of your life and the family and career-oriented second Major Cycle.

Transition periods always bring disruption to your personal relationships, career changes when necessary, pressure to make major decisions, and just about anything else that falls into the category of life's growing pains. You entered the Transition Period between the second Major Cycle of your life and your third Major Cycle during 1983 and you will be done with it in 1988. Just like the first Transition Period, things will not be easy, but you will survive the craziness if you are determined to do so. The years 1985 and 1986 will be the most difficult years of this Transition Period.

The turning point in your current nine-year cycle is 1986. This is a time to get rid of whatever obstacles you know are in your way. The most critical time for this is between January and May of this year. May through September of 1986 will be filled with opportunities to travel, enhance your love life, and promote financial growth. Although these opportunities will still be there if you procrastinate and avoid making necessary changes in your life, it will be very difficult to take advantage of them without running yourself ragged since you need to remove the known obstacles in your path before you can take advantage of these new opportunities.

So you must look at this year as a very important one because what you do during it will not only affect the next four years of your nine-year cycle, but it will have a great impact on what remains of your life. Since you are entering the third Major Cycle of your life, you need to give a lot of consideration to how you might go about fulfilling your destiny if you choose to do so.

Your destiny requires that you sensitize yourself to the universal human experiences so that you can show your awareness of these in forms that transcend any and all narrow-minded viewpoints. Your success depends on developing the instincts of the performer. You must learn to communicate your personal experiences with the comedy and drama of life in such a way as to help others survive physically, mentally, emotionally, and spiritually. Creativity is your main asset. Who you know can be as important as what you know since your opportunities are most likely to come through the people you have inspired. Allow life to be your stage and take advantage of any opportunity to get your message across to the public. Take care to discipline yourself. Take pains to master whatever you choose to promote or teach. Guard against the tendency to exaggerate and manipulate the truth. You will never lack for fans and their response to you will be gratifying; however, you need to acknowledge those people whose energy and loyalty supports the best within you if you are to truly leave this world a better place.

Your Life Challenge is the triple 0. This is the Challenge of the Old Soul and Responsibility. You cannot advance yourself without taking some responsibility for the growth of others on all levels. This does not mean that you should help others to your own detriment, however. If you do not take care of yourself, you will not have the energy to help others.

After going through the Numerology with Mr. P, I then took some time to center and ground again while I shuffled my tarot deck. Next I asked Mr. P if he had any particular concerns I should look into. He said he just wanted an idea of what to expect over the next six months. Then I had Mr. P cut the deck with his left hand three times and put the deck back into one pile any way he chose. Once I had the cards back in my hands, I laid out the Time Spread assigning the Time Period Cards a duration of one month each. The following is how the cards looked:

2 of Cups	3 of Pentacles	7 of Cups	10 of Wands	The Chariot	5 of Pentacles
		The Magician			
	The Fool	The Hierophant	The Tower	The Emperor	The High Priestess
Death					

After taking the time to allow my psychic senses to pick out the important patterns for this particular reading, this is how I put it all together.

Mr. P, the central issue for you over the next six months is represented by The Magician. This means that you will need to exercise your will in order to accomplish whatever you choose to do. It sounds simple, but it isn't. When I look at the cards representing your psychological inventory (Death, The Fool, and The Hierophant) I see a man divided against himself. One part of you understands and welcomes the life-changing events that are coming your way. Another part of you foolishly ignores what is necessary at this time. Finally there is a part of you which is used to being in charge and prefers things to remain stable at a time when change is important. In order to exercise your will and cooperate with the life-changing potential we acknowledged in your Numerology chart, you will need some outside help. The card of The High Priestess represents a female person of great knowledge who could counsel you wisely if you let her. From the looks of this spread, you are not likely to seek out her advice. I suggest that you reconsider. If you do not change any of your patterns, then the month of January will be full of difficulties. There will seem to be too many things to do in any given day and very little financial reward for the work that you must do. February will bring an opportunity to travel and get away from some of the difficulties at home. However, if you make the mistake of stirring up a hornets' nest in the northern city you visit, the trip will not prove as rejuvenating as it should. March brings some unexpected expenses. Check now to see if any appliances, residences, or vehicles are in need of repair which will be less expensive now than they will be if you wait three months. April shows you fighting with yourself due to an old and debilitating addiction. The demand that you repay an old debt through the use of your special skills gives you temporary lucrative employment and a very good reason to pull yourself together during May. June continues this employment and brings you into contact with a lady who will first be a friendly acquaintance and then a lover.

Mr. P, it looks to me as if you really need to change some of what is likely to go on in your life over the next few months. The use of your will to avoid flirting with an old addiction could save you a lot of trouble. The demands on you from people in foreign governments during May might not be entirely avoidable, but if you are in good shape when the demands are made, you should be able to negotiate a deal more to your liking. This doesn't appear to be an issue over money. Rather it seems your self-respect is on the line.

Once this reading was done, I talked with Mr. P for quite a while. He identified with the reading from the Numerology chart and the one from the tarot cards. He was having trouble reaching his potential and there was a part of him that was very depressed about that. Unfortunately, as is often the case, having information and doing something productive with it are two very different things. Mr. P did not avoid his bout with addiction, he caused great difficulties during his February trip, and he did indeed work off a debt to a foreign military agency, but this gave him no sense of satisfaction other than monetary. The romance also developed, but it was hard for Mr. P to really trust another human being.

Mr. P was out of touch with me after this reading. I later heard that in the spring of 1993 he decided he'd had enough of life and chose to stop taking the medicine he needed to keep him alive. What I found saddest was that he never seemed to realize how big a difference he made in the lives of those around him. Ironically, he made his biggest contribution to the growth of others when he wasn't worrying about how to make his mark in the world. Perhaps he fulfilled his destiny in spite of himself.

The reason I chose to record Mr. P's last reading is because it combines success with loss. If you choose to develop your psychic potential to the degree that allows you to do readings of this kind, you will have to accept the fact that some clients will choose what seems to be a self-defeating path. All you can do is relay the information to them, make recommendations, and work with them while you can. Not everyone, and perhaps not even the majority will choose to do the work which is in their best interests. You will see this behavior in intelligent and gifted people like Mr. P and in more ordinary types who simply cannot see beyond the narrow confines of their everyday lives, such as the woman who tells you she can't leave the man who beats her because she "loves" him.

Now go back over both the Numerology reading and the tarot reading and see if you can follow the patterns that lead to the conclusions that I made. After you have worked through these readings for a second or even third time, try a combination Numerology and tarot reading for a friend or relative. Remember to center and ground, let your psychic senses focus on the most important elements within the chart or spread, and then use your intellect to analyze the result.

CHAPTER 9

THE WORLD NEEDS YOU
AT YOUR BEST!

OFTEN I AM ASKED WHY I believe it is important for people to develop their psychic potential. My answer is simple. Psychic abilities are part of our human abilities. If they go undeveloped or are developed in an unbalanced manner, we cheat ourselves, humanity, the world, and our Creator by not being the best people we can be.

There has never been a time in our history when it was so important to use our human abilities to their fullest. Change is rapid these days. We are in extreme need of highly developed intuition to avoid destroying ourselves and our planet with what we think of as progress.

I have been blessed by teachers who knew how to get this message across to me in no uncertain terms. One of my obligations as their student is to pass their message along. In the following paragraphs I will share with you a little more about what two of them thought was important.

My first teacher was the late Grandmaster of Pai Lum Kung Fu, Daniel K. Pai. I recently wrote the following article for the benefit of my martial arts family.

Choosing Growth on the Warrior's Path

Once in a great while, my teacher (Pai Lum's Grandmaster Daniel K. Pai) would tell me a little about his early training. He said he was taught things "backwards." The killing stroke of a sword, knife, hand, foot, or any one of a dozen different mundane tools that could also become weapons was where his training started. It was only later that anything approaching a structure building up to the ability to execute, control, use, and/or abuse these techniques was shown to him. His initial training in the martial arts was not meant to be health-building, nor was it meant to be recreational. It was intended to increase his chance of survival as he served first his family as a "bill collector," and later his country as a soldier (Korea and Vietnam). What we know as basics may have been beaten into him early on, but only as a means of insuring that he became an effective weapon in his grandfather's or country's arsenal. My teacher's survival training was important to both his family and country simply because it was a more efficient use of their resources to keep him alive and useful during his physical prime than it would have been to use him up prematurely.

Sounds like a very hard way to live! Daniel K. Pai learned how to survive, but more importantly he learned how to learn. However, since he learned tactics, strategy, and technique in what he termed a "backwards" (read: "survival-oriented") manner; the categories and structures associated with so-called traditional training in the Asian martial arts (as taught at various commercial dojos and schools in this country) simply weren't particularly important to him until he found himself running a number of commercial martial arts schools over the years. This is one of the reasons that the task of systematizing Pai Lum training was left to Grandmaster Pai's senior students (the original second generation grandchildren) as part of their obligation to Pai Lum and their teacher.

My teacher was the epitome of what legend calls a Warrior. Altering his course from living as a "soldier," serving someone else's cause, to becoming a "Warrior" was a choice that Daniel K. Pai made sometime after he realized that he had survived his initial obligations to family and country (something I doubt either his family or country expected him to do). Later in his life this decision was supplemented with the further choice to teach what he had learned under the names of Pai Lum, White Dragon Fist, Fire Dragon, White Lotus, and Bok Leen Pai. As far as I can tell, only Pai Lum was really more than a "business name" to him.

Not being legally able to train students in the same manner as he was taught, my teacher developed his own ways. I don't pretend to understand all that he did, nor why. I simply know what I experienced and what my brothers have shared with me of their experiences with Grandmaster Daniel K. Pai. Like my teacher before me, there are some methods of training which I experienced that I do not choose to use with my students. Like him, I sought alternatives to provide myself and my students with the necessary training that would allow access to the Warrior's Path.

Quite a number of years ago I came across a description of ancient Budo teachings in Shihan Fred Lovret's magazine, *The Bujin* (Winter Issue 1982–1983). According to Ginchen Funakoshi (originally quoted from *Karate Nijuka-jo* as translated by Masahito Nishida), there are three stages through which the Budoka (student of the Warrior Arts) must pass. They are the following:

1. *Shu*—Guarding and keeping the basic tenets of one's first teacher: Mastering one style.

2. *Ha*—Seeking other areas of training and understanding about the Warrior Arts.

3. *Ri*—Departing from the study of the methods of others and creating one's own style.

These three stages were recognized in the past as a *must* for those who would truly walk the Path of the Warrior. In the present, however, both students and their teachers often attempt to arrest development at one of the first two stages. This can only lead to frustration and disillusionment on both sides of the student/teacher relationship.

This error can and often is compounded by misinterpreting the obligation of the teacher to the student which the Japanese call *Giri*. Shihan F. J. Lovret interprets *Giri* as meaning that "a sensei (teacher) must never admit to a lack of knowledge" (*The Bujin*, Winter Issue 1982–1983). He qualifies this statement by adding that a sensei should not "go around claiming to know everything." Giri then is the teacher's obligation to his/her student to provide the knowledge that that student requires. Since no one teacher will know everything there is to know about the martial arts, never mind everything there is to know about everything, there will be times when the teacher must put to good use his/her ability to *learn*. If a teacher does not personally know something a particular student needs to know, he/she is obligated to research and learn it, or provide the student with an alternative way to access the necessary information.

So what happens to both student and teach both of them attempt to limit development alor rior's Path to the first two stages listed above?

1. If progress is limited to Stage 1:

A. The student who masters the first style he is taught (assuming that no one style of martial arts encompasses *all* of martial knowledge, technique, and wisdom) will feel frustrated by the slowdown of further training forthcoming from his/her teacher. This often forces the beginning of Stage 2. The student in this case will develop a guilty conscience, accuse his/her teacher of being inadequate in some way, and break away from his first teacher and style. Thus begins the quest for the impossible, a teacher who truly knows everything about everything.

B. The teacher who develops a master-level student and doesn't encourage "post graduate studies" limits the potential progress of his more junior students through the rank structure, incites revolt, and ends up playing politics with his master-level students who don't have the "good sense" to be exactly alike. Ultimately this attitude limits all potential for the future growth and evolution of the teacher's style of martial arts. That which does not grow and/or change, is dead!

2. If progress is limited to Stage 2:

A. The student who has mastered his first style of martial arts and has sought out supplementary training eventually reaches the point where he/she must systematize what he knows in order to pass it on to his/her students in an efficient manner. It will become clear to a master-level student at this point that at least his/her style of teaching will necessarily be different in some ways from that of his/her first teacher's. If these differences are not allowed to be used and passed on, the master-level student will backslide to the first stage of development and will never use his/her creative ability to improve his/her first teacher's style. (Not all students will be able to do this, but it should be the goal for the most serious students to work toward using their energy to the betterment of their first teacher's style.)

B. The teacher who has prompted a master-level student to seek out supplementary training in the martial arts, but tries to keep him/her from evolving his/her own manner of expressing this compound knowledge, locks himself/herself into a game of: "Will the real master of this style please stand up?" This game will divide the loyalties of the junior students and create greater political problems than would have developed if the teacher had arrested the development of his/her master-level student to Stage 1. Ultimately the teacher's style of martial arts will devolve rather than evolve over time.

The choices listed above boil down to either walking the Warrior's Path and leading your students to do so, or not. This should not be taken to mean that every student who thinks he is a master and capable of starting his own style should do so, however. In fact, great care must be taken to evaluate your behavior as either a student, or teacher, or both. "Know thyself" is the charge of the successful Warrior. Growth in the martial arts is a continuous process and cannot be successfully confined. The problems that provide the plots for many "Kung Fu" movies (ego-related misuse of power, prestige, and politics) are avoidable. Students should be encouraged to maximize their development for the honor and future development of their first teacher's style. Teachers should strive to inspire at least one student to exceed the teacher's capabilities and understanding in the areas of martial technique, mental control, and philosophy of living well.

The alternative is stagnation. This is a terminal disease in any martial art. It is certainly more lethal than any threat that an occasional student will get carried away with himself/herself and become only a "legend in his/her own mind." (This expression was coined by Shihan Vincent Ward of Allentown, PA.) Creative thinking is what distinguishes the leader from the follower and the warrior from the soldier. It is to be valued in all walks of life. To deliberately discourage this trait in one's students, due to fear or egotism, is the greatest sacrilege a teacher can commit!

Everything that I have said in the above article about growth on the Warrior's Path might equally well have been said about growth in any area of human potential. Daniel K. Pai had a highly developed intuition and intellect. He always told me that both were essential to a successful life.

Wm. G. Gray was both a teacher and a colleague to me. He was very serious about living a life of spirituality while working for the betterment of humanity in this world. This cannot be done without developing your God-given gifts to their fullest. One of the hardest things to do in this world is to truly *know* what is good for humanity over the long run. So many new inventions in the realms of technology, pharmacology, etc., are cropping up so quickly that we cannot help but be confused by the possibilities for the future. Only developing a working relationship with Divinity will help us discern what leads to constructive growth and what leads to destructive devolution before it is too late to do anything about the path we are on. Since relating to Divinity requires us to work through our spiritual faculties, these must be developed fully for the best results.

Since the beginning of this book I have been teaching you how to develop, focus, and use your psychic abilities in a manner consistent with good psychological health. One of the final things that you must learn has the function of helping you maintain your sanity as your powers grow. In this book's early chapters I suggested that it was important to remember that even the strongest psychic impression can be interpreted in the wrong way. Reminding yourself on a regular basis that you can be *wrong* is very important to your mental health. In fact there may even be times when you are asked to intuit an answer to a question when you simply *don't know* the answer. Accepting this as a real possibility will help you deal sanely with the times when it is an actuality.

Many intelligent and gifted people for some reason are not interested in being directed mentally, psychically, or spiritually. This is generally because they assume that they are perfectly capable of directing themselves. If you fall into this unfortunate manner of thinking about yourself, you will have a very hard time realizing how important the information in the paragraph above truly is to you until you make at least one big mistake. That is why I strongly advise you to find someone who is psychic and has more experience than you do in either spiritual matters or just plain sane living to act as your "supervisor." Doing so will help you avoid creating a major or minor disaster in your life or in someone else's.

The person you choose as a psychic supervisor must be willing to listen to what has been going on in your life and your work as a psychic (especially if you work as a professional psychic), ask penetrating questions when it is clear that you are deluding yourself or otherwise getting into hot water, and must be someone you trust and respect. You will find that most therapists participate in a similar type of supervision as do most people who devote themselves to a particular spiritual path within one of the organized religions. There is a good reason for this practice.

Developing your special abilities, whether they be psychic, spiritual, intellectual, or a combination of all three, leaves you vulnerable to also developing an artificially inflated ego. If you get a "swelled head" about your powers, you may easily end up manipulating others and fooling yourself. At the very least, this behavior is useless and at worst, it is disruptive to your life on all levels. As we have seen, the mind, body, psychic abilities, and soul of a human being are very closely linked to each other. Impairment to any one of these parts of you can have a draining effect on all of the others.

Now ask yourself this question, "Who sees his own errors clearly all the time?" The truthful answer is, "No one." This is the reason each of us needs some form of psychic supervision and/or spiritual direction on a regular basis in order to maintain our overall sanity.

The need for psychic supervision will become all the more clear as you meet people who have developed their psychic potential on their own. Some of these people will seem to be near genius level in the development of their psychic abilities. Unfortunately, many of these psychics will also often be bizarre in their behavior and attitudes towards other humans and life in general. Some will think nothing of using their powers to get whatever they want. These same people often decide to psychically influence authority figures in order to gain special treatment for themselves, or they may seek attention by putting on a "psychic show" (instigating poltergeist activity for instance). None of this behavior, whether it is acted out intentionally or subconsciously, is particularly productive in the long run and most of it is merely selfish abuse of power.

Developing a sound relationship with your psychic supervisor will not only help you keep on the straight and narrow ethically, but it will help you develop the skills you need when you are ready to provide supervision for others. Among other benefits, you will find out that the keys to progress in most fields of endeavor are discipline, persistence, and humility. During your association with your psychic supervisor, you will also come to realize that the best psychics are distinguished by their practical attitudes toward life.

Psychics, intellectuals, and mystics are all peculiarly subject to delusions, especially those involving self-importance. Discipline and humility can best be ensured within the framework of some organized set of rules. One of the first things that you should establish in conjunction with your psychic supervisor is a reasonable and simple set of rules that you, as a psychic, agree to live by. These rules are not supposed to be a bludgeon your supervisor can use every time you get out of line, and you will occasionally. On the contrary, the rules are there to remind you of the standards that you consider appropriate for honorable men and women with developed psychic abilities.

The rules you lay out for yourself will become a set of tools that your psychic supervisor can use to help you maintain your balance. For instance, if you told your psychic supervisor that you had been at a social gathering where you found yourself reading tarot cards for a number of people, you might very well be asked the following questions, all based on a rule you had developed concerning the inadvisability of manipulating others solely for your own benefit:

1. Why did you bring tarot cards to a party?

2. Were the other people at the gathering already aware that you are a practicing psychic?

3. Were you asked to do the readings, or did you offer?

4. What did you get in return for the tarot card readings? Approval? Awe? A date?

Now it might very well be that you were known by everyone as a psychic and the host of the party had asked you to bring your cards along. In this case, unless you set out to procure romantic interest for yourself by your performance, you were acting within the "letter of the law" so to speak. However, your psychic supervisor might still suggest that you think very hard about why you were willing to provide entertainment with your rather exceptional abilities. In other words, what did you get out of it? What did you learn?

As you continue your work as a psychic, you will refine your set of rules. But the following is the simplest rule you could choose to live by although it may very well be the hardest to consistently live up to: *First, do no harm!*

In closing, I would like to recall once again the words of Medicine Chief James O'Loughlin—you are all perfect right now for whatever time, place, and circumstances you find yourself in. Developing your psychic abilities to improve yourself, the world, and the future of humanity is important. During a recent public lecture in Flanders, New Jersey, Chief O'Loughlin said that the future was bringing great change and that his type of knowledge would be needed greatly by the rest of humanity. That is why he has been willing to share with everyone knowledge that was once known only to his people. It is for the same reason that I have shared my knowledge of psychic development with you.

ADDITIONAL RESOURCES

Martial Arts and Sensitivity Training available from these senior teachers associated with Pai Lum Kung Fu

Pai Li-Lung (John Weninger)
160 East Moorestown Rd.
Wind Gap, PA 18091
Phone: (610) 759-0828
e-mail: lilung@pailum.com

Pai Ching-Lin (David L. Smith)
Pai Shou Athletic Association
P.O. Box 371
New London, CT 06320
e-mail: paichinglin@bigfoot.com

Pai Pai-He (Marcia L. Pickands)
White Lotus Temple
3 Burhans Place
Delmar, NY 12054
e-mail: paipaihe@AOL.com

Pai Hsin-Lung (Phil Hunter)
P.O. Box 298
Climax, NC 27233
e-mail: Hsin Lung@AOL.com

Pai Shin Zan (Thomas D. St. Charles)
21 Donna Ave.
Derby, CT 06418

Pai Ying (Robert Skaling)
86 Fulton St.
Keyport, NJ 07735

Pai Lung-Shi (Dr. Ed Strok)
e-mail: lungshi@ns.sympatico.ca

Cherokee teachers, elders, and spiritual leaders who are available to the public

Mom Feather—Elder and Spiritual Leader
e-mail: MOMFEATHR@AOL.com

Yona Gadoga (Standing Bear)—Teacher
e-mail: YONAGADOGA@AOL.com

Walks With Old Ones—Medicine Chief
Contact Yonagadoga and ask for a consultation.

Sangreal Sodality
Marcia L. Pickands, Warden
Sangreal Sodality
3 Burhans Place
Delmar, NY 12054

BIBLIOGRAPHY

Bishop, Barbara J. *Numerology: Universal Vibrations of Numbers*. St. Paul, MN: Llewellyn Publications, 1990.

Carrington, H. *Your Psychic Powers and How to Develop Them*. North Hollywood, CA: Newcastle Publishing, 1975.

Connolly, Eileen. *The Connolly Tarot, Volumes I and II*. North Hollywood, CA: Newcastle Publishing, 1987.

Friedlander, J. and Pearson, C. *The Practical Psychic*. York Beach, ME: Samuel Weiser, 1993.

Garen, Nancy. *Tarot Made Easy*. New York: Simon & Schuster, 1989.

Goodwin, Matthew O. *Numerology: The Complete Guide, Volumes I and II*. North Hollywood, CA: Newcastle Publishing, 1981.

Gordon, David. *Therapeutic Metaphors*. Cupertino, CA: Meta Publications, 1978.

Gray, Wm. G. *The Sangreal Tarot*. York Beach, ME: Samuel Weiser, 1988.

———. *Western Inner Workings*. York Beach, ME: Samuel Weiser, 1983.

Hammond, D. *Handbook of Hypnotic Suggestions and Metaphors*. New York: W. W. Norton & Company, 1990.

Hewitt, W. *Hypnosis*. St. Paul, MN: Llewellyn Publications, 1987.

———. *Beyond Hypnosis*. St. Paul, MN: Llewellyn Publications, 1987.

Huson, P. *Mastering Witchcraft: A Practical Guide for Witches, Warlocks, and Covens*. New York: Putnam, 1970.

Johnson, V. and Wommack, T. *The Secrets of Numbers*. York Beach, ME: Samuel Weiser, 1982.

Knight, G. *The Magical World of the Tarot*. York Beach, ME: Samuel Weiser, 1996.

Lingerman, H. A. *The Book of Numerology*. York Beach, ME: Samuel Weiser, 1994.

Nichols, S. *Jung and Tarot*. York Beach, ME: Samuel Weiser, 1980.

Payne, Phoebe and Bendit, Laurence. *The Psychic Sense*. New York: E. P. Dutton, 1949.

Pickands, Marcia. *The Psychic Self-Defense Personal Training Manual*. York Beach, ME: Samuel Weiser, 1997.

Rice, P. and Rice, V. *Potential*. York Beach, ME: Samuel Weiser, 1987.

Sherwood, Keith. *The Art of Spiritual Healing*. St. Paul, MN: Llewellyn Publications, 1992.

Wang, R. *Qabalistic Tarot*. York Beach, ME: Samuel Weiser, 1983.

White, John W. *Frontiers of Consciousness: The Meeting Ground Between Inner and Outer Reality*. New York: Julian Press, 1974.

Yeterian, Dixie. *Exploring Psychic Reality: Discovering Your Extrasensory Gifts*. New York: Crown Publishers, 1975.

INDEX

alphabet, 35
awareness, awakening, 6

Birth Name Chart, 34
Birthdate chart, 37
body, invisible, 77
Budoka, 117

centering, 4
ceremonial practice, 85
communicating with the
    dead, 63
conscious awareness, 10
conscious minds, 11
Current Trend Spread, 20

daily reading, 19
Destiny number, 41
discarnate entities, 65, 66
Disney Tarot, 14
divination, 54, 55, 56, 62
    tarot, 59
Divinity, relationship with,
    45, 50
dreams, prophetic, 10
Dumb Supper, 65, 71

foresight, 11

Gray, William G., 51, 85, 121
grounding, 5

Initiation of the Cup, 85
intuitive impressions, 106
invocation, midday, 53

journal, 51

languages, symbolic, 12, 13,
    27
Lovret, Shihan F. J., 118

Major Arcana, 14
Masahito Nishida, 117
materialism, exploitative, 84
meditation, morning, 53
Minor Arcana, 14
Morgan Greer deck, 14
Motherpeace deck, 14

numbers, meaning of, 28
numerology, 27
    major cycles of, 38

Ouija board, 63, 65, 66, 67
    using, 67
O'Loughlin, Chief James, 2,
    49, 125

Pai, Daniel K., 2, 115
perfect, being, 2
power, temptation of, 50

psychic abilities, 1, 3, 43
  advanced applications of, 105
  responsible use of, 77
psychic body, stretching out, 80
psychic readings, 55
psychic supervisor, 122, 123

quest, nightly, 53

Rider-Waite deck, 14

Sacred Rose deck, 14
scrying, 85
seances, 63, 65
see, learning to, 9
senses, five physical, 3
Shakespearean Tarot, 14
soul, immortality of, 63
spirit guides, 66
spirits of the dead, 74

spiritual power, 43
standards, ethical, 84
strength testing, 79
study, evening, 53
subconscious mind, 10
symbols, 11

tarot cards, 13, 56
  choosing, 14
  meaning of individual, 15, 16
  reading for others, 24
time, psychically sensing, 8
Time Spread, 19, 21
trance medium, 66

Vision Quest, 47
  accelerated, 48

warrior's path, 115
Wilkes, Brian Standing Bear, 9, 47

Marcia L. Pickands is a remarkably versatile teacher with training in psychology, theology, ceremonial magic, and many other esoteric, metaphysical and magical topics. In addition to her twenty-nine years experience as a psychic and spiritual adviser, and her twenty-two years as a mother, she has worked as an archaeological technician, an historic artifact analyst, a New Age bookstore owner, a Neo-Pagan High Priestess, and a martial arts master and teacher. She is one of the two spiritual successors to the late William G. Gray, renowned author of many fine books on magic and the Western Inner Tradition, and serves as the Warden of the Sangreal Sodality. In addition, Ms. Pickands is the current Senior Master of the Guardians, a Warrior-Priest Order dedicated to preserving, protecting, and promoting the Way of Light within this world by doing Good and averting Evil.